A Po

A POCKETBOOK
OF
WELSH HOUSE-NAMES

Edwin C. Lewis

Copyright © 2004 Edwin C. Lewis

Published in 2004 by
Cyhoeddwyr Dinefwr Publishers
Rawlings Road, Llandybie
Carmarthenshire, SA18 3YD

The right of Edwin C. Lewis to be identified as the Author of the Work
has been asserted by him in accordance with the
Copyright, Designs and Patents Act 1988.

*All rights reserved. No part of this publication may be reproduced, stored
in a retrieval system or transmitted, in any form or by any means without
the prior permission of the publisher, nor be otherwise circulated in any
form of binding or cover other than that in which it is published and
without similar condition being imposed on the subsequent purchaser.*

A CIP catalogue record for this book is
available from the British Library.

ISBN 1-904323-06-5

Printed and bound in Wales by
Dinefwr Press Ltd.
Rawlings Road, Llandybie
Carmarthenshire, SA18 3YD

I Mer

ACKNOWLEDGEMENTS

I wish to thank Gwasg Dinefwr Press Ltd., the publishers of *Y Geiriadur Cryno – The Concise Welsh Dictionary* (2001), which I edited, for permission to include the section on Welsh Pronunciation in this work.

Further, I must express my gratitude to Mr Ioan Evans, B.Eng., for his skill and patience in typing and setting my original manuscript in its present form for publication.

E.C.L.

PREFACE

A Pocketbook of Welsh House-Names is concerned with the presentation, classification and interpretation of a comprehensive collection of Welsh house-names mostly in current use.

Census returns, electoral rolls, telephone directories, parish registers, Welsh hymn-books, family notices in national and local newspapers, Tithe maps, conveyancing documents, commemorative inscriptions together with the Royal Mail's *Postal Address Book* have all been scrutinised as supplementary sources. However, the primary source of Welsh house-names must be the very dwellings themselves. The names remain exhibited above or beside front doors, on entrance pillars, walls, posts and gates from Trefdraeth to Trefynwy and from Llanfair Pwllgwyngyll to Llangyfelach. Long may the tradition flourish!

E.C.L.

Dôl-helyg,
Rhydargaeau,
Carmarthen.

CONTENTS

PREFACE	vii
INTRODUCTION	1
The ethos of Welsh house-names	2
Welsh house-names derived from place-names	3
Descriptive Welsh house-names	4
Welsh house-names that extol the concept of 'home'	7
House-names and personal identity	8
Shop-names	9
Historical occasions and house-names	11
Fashionable house-names	11
Welsh house-names – a major difference	12
A house by any other name . . .	13
Welsh public house-names	15
Welsh house-names and Welsh hymn-tunes	16
'I name this house . . .'	16
Signs of the times	17
Welsh house-names and the future	18
References	20
LIST OF WELSH HOUSE-NAMES	23
PRONUNCIATION	145
GLOSSARY	151
SELECT BIBLIOGRAPHY	157

INTRODUCTION

Lovely the woods, waters, meadows, combes, vales,
All the air things wear that build this world of Wales . . .
Gerard Manley Hopkins

THE three greatest assets of Wales are its language, its landscape and its people. That these impinge upon each other in this collection of Welsh house-names is no coincidence. Language in this connection is used succinctly, descriptively, poetically and at times humorously. Landscape is deeply etched by regional reference to mountains, hills, valleys, ridges, passes, rivers, lakes, springs, coastline, forests, fields, flora and fauna. Welsh people in spirit are as indomitable as ever. From the Age of Saints (*Oes y Saint*) to the recent setting-up of the National Assembly for Wales (*Cynulliad Cenedlaethol Cymru*) their zealous passion for religion, radicalism, recollection (and rugby) remains. The house-names continue to reflect this kaleidoscope of colour, consciousness and character.

The ethos of Welsh house-names:

Welsh house-names have about them a pervading aura of charm, mystery and distinctiveness. They are not solely what they purport to be. Some speak poignantly of a time when the Welsh language flourished throughout the land, and yet remain an integral part of the living language today. Many of them recall a long forgotten age, a few echo local folklore, others refer to a pre-industrial era and several have strong connections with the recent past. There are also those that encapsulate the immediacy of the moment and appear ageless. All are inextricably woven into the rich tapestry of the history, language and literature of Wales.

A study of the Welsh house-names of an area can frequently provide the social historian with a rich source of primary material. Insights and terms of reference may be derived regarding the topography of a district and valuable clues discovered in connection with the nature or origin of the residence, past or present. Welsh house-names can often supplement the meagre details of recorded history.

Whether from the mining valleys of the South, the slate-quarrying districts of the North, the coastal ports of the West or the rural villages of Mid-Wales, Welsh house-names may be generally classified into three main groups:

(i) House-names derived from place-names,

(ii) Descriptive house-names,

(iii) House-names that extol the concept of 'home'.

Welsh house-names derived from place-names:

Examples of place-names transferred as house-names abound everywhere and are not a peculiarly Welsh feature. The names of rivers, hills and mountains are usually considered to be the oldest names in existence. No other group of names can rival their primordial ranking. Initially, a place did not possess a name but merely a description. In early times, places could and frequently did change their names, the same was not true of rivers, hills and mountains. Theirs were of a more permanent nature.[1]

House-names in this group may refer back to the place of origin of a family or to the birthplace of one of the former occupants of the dwelling. During the nineteenth century many people moved from the rural areas to the industrialised valleys of the South and some brought with them the names of their native heaths: **Aberdaron, Berwyn, Carn Ingli, Ceredigion, Tre-fin, Yr Wyddfa . . .** There are place-names adapted as house-names because of nostalgic memories of past holidays, linguistic souvenirs as it were: **Clarach, Gŵyr, Porth-cawl, Trefor, Y Barri, Y Sgeti . . .**

A significant chapter of Welsh history is connected with two particular groups of place-names of foreign origin, which have been transferred as house-names in Wales. Emigration had been a feature of Welsh life for centuries. Thousands of Welsh people had moved across Offa's Dyke to England, more by far had crossed the Atlantic to North America. One great wave of emigration began around 1817 and finally peaked after the period called the 'hungry forties'. Poverty, religious oppression and landlordism were the main evils responsible for such massive movements of population. By 1857, it was reputed that there was not, 'a single one (in South Wales), who had not either a father, brother, son, uncle, nephew, cousin, or at least some near friend in America'.[2] A mixture of pride and *hiraeth* in the hearts of the relatives who remained in Wales precipitated the use of new house-names which identified the residence and the resident with the emigrant, the entrepreneur who had ventured westward in quest of work or a better life.[3] The new house-names were: **Baltimore, Boston, Denver, Pennsylvania, Philadelphia, Pittsburgh** . . . Then again, by July 1865, the first Welsh settlers had arrived on the shores of Patagonia. Some 2,000 more were to follow eventually. Hopes of establishing a Welsh Colony in Argentina were beginning to crystallise and confidence in the venture was reflected in the appearance of such novel house-names as: **Camwy, Chubut, Gaiman, Patagonia, Y Wladfa** . . .

Descriptive Welsh house-names:

In this group of names reference is frequently made to the position, size, colour, age, occupant, former use or past history of a dwelling. Fine views are sometimes extolled, as are specific locations, settings or aspects. On occasions, a house-name may appear stark and austere, and reveal only the briefest of details regarding the dwelling: **Dan-y-bryn, Ger-y-coed, Penyrheol, Tŷ-calch, Tŷ-coch, Tyddyn-uchaf, Tŷ-mawr, Tynewydd, Ty'n celyn, Y Bwthyn, Y Felin** . . . Such examples may well be a direct response to the need for a short, straightforward, self-explanatory name, as in: **Awelon, Glanyrafon, Llwyn-**

helyg, Nant-oer, Pen-y-bryn, Tŷ-canol, Ty'nlôn, Tŷ'r-capel, Tŷ-cerrig, Y Deri . . . Sometimes, however, language is used differently, and even though the same requirements are addressed, that is, of position, size, colour, age, situation, views, etc., the names involved have about them a distinctively lyrical quality and are evocative and expressive, as shown by: **Adlais-y-don, Allt-y-gog, Brig-y-don, Bron-y-wawr, Huanfa, Llety'r Bugail, Llety-cariad, Llwyn-yr-haf, Llygad-yr-haul, Llys-yr-wylan, Min-yr-awel, Mysg-y-meysydd, Nant-y-clychau, Sain-yr-ehedydd** . . . Then again, names such as: **Oceana, Almora, Resolute, Amity, Europa, Asiana** . . . appear as house-names in some Welsh coastal villages and ports. The names themselves are those of merchant ships, and their transference as house-names stems from the rigorous seafaring tradition that flourished along the coast of Wales well into the first decades of the twentieth century. Often the master of a vessel would take his ship's name with him upon retiring from the sea, as it would have been a substantial part of his personal identity during the heyday of his maritime career. Retirement would not be allowed to rob him entirely of this status, as his new address would proclaim. He would continue to be hailed as 'Captain Lloyd, **Arethusa**, Cliff Terrace . . .' more distinctive by far than merely 'Captain Lloyd of **Ivy-cottage**' or '. . . of **Sea-view**'. In much the same context, there is the related example where anonymity and reflected glory tinge the descriptive house-name: **Tŷ'r Capten**.

Personal names are also evident among Welsh house-names and usually refer to the dwelling's occupant, past or present: **Bryn Myrddin, Ffos Anna, Llys Ifor, Tŷ**

Elfed, Tŷ Glyn, Tŷ Gwilym, Tŷ Mair, Tŷ Twmi, Tyddyn Meilir . . .[5] On occasions, a family relationship is implied, as in **Tŷ Tad-cu, Tŷ Taid** and **Tŷ Ni**.

Names of animals and birds feature frequently in Welsh house-names. The animals named, whether domesticated or wild, are usually those found in neighbouring fields and woodlands, such as: horse, goat, sheep, squirrel, pig, deer, fox, hedgehog, otter, mouse . . . Examples abound: **Allt-y-cadno, Allt-y-geifr, Allt-y-perchyll, Bryn-ceffylau, Cae'r march, Corlan-y-defaid, Corn-Gafr, Craig-y-wiwer, Dôl-y-cadno, Dwrgi-bach, Gwâl-yr-hwch, Llety-llygoden, Llys-y-draenog** . . .

Names of birds are popular and well represented among Welsh house-names. The birds listed range from the tiny wren to the mighty eagle and include the gull, duck, falcon, cockerel, cuckoo, swallow, lark, crow, magpie . . . and give rise to such house-names as: **Blaen-nant-yr-hebog, Bro-hedydd, Bryn-hedydd, Cae'r gog, Cae'r wylan, Colomendy, Cri'r wylan, Cwm-y-frân, Llwyn-eos, Llwyn-llinos, Llwyn-yr-eos, Nyth-y-dryw, Nyth-y-frân, Llys-y-wennol, Llys-yr-wylan, Sain-yr-ehedydd** . . .

Of more recent origin is the practice of blending part of the husband's name with that of the wife's and then of labelling the house with the hybrid form. Glyndwr and Wendy live happily at **Glynwen**, whereas Dorothy and Anthony dwell serenely at **Dorant**. Elwyn and Alice could well raise a few eyebrows if they resided at **El-Al**, whilst one possible consolation in merging Llwyd with Brenda would be **Llwybren**. Perhaps Penrhyn and Olwen would be well advised to decide upon a more conventional form of name for their home!

Welsh house-names that extol the concept of 'home':

In Wales, as in many countries, the houses best preserved over the centuries have usually been those of the rich and powerful. That such buildings have survived the ravages of time and weather in far greater numbers than the poorly constructed cottages and small houses of *y Werin*, the vast majority of the population of Wales, is not to be wondered at. Yet in many ways these small properties 'actually have more to tell us *en masse* about the lives of our ancestors than the relatively few great houses that were ever built in Wales.'[6] These small dwellings, along with others, would certainly have been endowed with house-names by at least the beginning of the nineteenth century. The Tithe Maps (*Mapiau'r Degwm*) chronicle much of this information from 1835 onwards. The Census Returns of 1841 further show that by then the custom was well established.

It would appear that all the house-names contained in this group seem to exemplify the truth expressed in the old maxim, 'Home is where the heart is.' **Cartref** (literally: *home*) is the most popular of all Welsh house-names and is proudly displayed in every corner of the country.[7] To some, home may be seen as a resting place after the long day's toil, a retreat from the busy bustling world, a place of quietness, serenity and beauty, a safe anchorage, a refuge, a sanctuary or shelter from life's tempestuous storms. To others, home, sweet home, may be considered as *the* ultimate goal to make for. To most people the attributes of home are incomparably satisfying, embracing hearth and family, a realm in which the young are nurtured, the old cherished and where love abides. There is little wonder, therefore, that the tranquillity of the ideal home embodies the very joys, comforts and virtues of paradise itself. Typical names in this group include: **Argel, Angorfa, Arhosfan, Clydfan, Delfan, Dihangfa, Gorffwysfa, Hyfrydle, Noddfa, Pen-y-daith, Tawelfan, Tegfan, Tŷ-ni, Yr Aelwyd, Y Gilfach-glyd, Y Gorlan, Y Nyth, Bodlondeb, Gwynfa, Paradwys...**

House-names and personal identity:

A great variety of Welsh house-names exists and this has brought some benefits in its wake. Nowadays people are usually identified by their names: Meurig Gruffydd, Aled Llywelyn, Gwen Owain, Illtud Prydderch, Ioan Tudur . . . There was a time in the past, more so in England, when people would often have been known for what they were by what they did: Joan Cook, Francis Cooper, George Miller, John Shepherd, Henry Smith, William Weaver . . . In medieval Wales a man identified himself by declaring that he was 'the son of someone', as in, '*Ifan ap Gronw ap Tegid ap Gwynfryn ap Madog ap Rhys ap Rhodri . . .*' (Ifan son of Gronw son of Tegid son of Gwynfryn son of Madog son of Rhys son of Rhodri . . .) In England there are examples of a similar pattern, the surname refers to but one generation, as in Clarkson, Davidson, Gilbertson, Johnson, Richardson, Williamson . . . It was in the period from the beginning of the sixteenth century to the middle of the nineteenth century that the Welsh people acquired settled surnames.[8] The outcome was confusing to say the least, as is manifested by the proliferation of such surnames as

Jones, Evans, Davies, Thomas and Williams. That unrelated persons living in small communities and sharing similar surnames should choose similar Christian names exacerbated a situation which had already become critical. It was then that the Welsh house-name proved to be doubly useful. It gave to the dwelling itself a particular reference, and to the occupant an element of uniqueness. The proverbial John Jones could at last be easily distinguished from his namesakes, for he would be greeted as 'John Jones, **Glanyrafon**', as opposed to 'John Jones, **Tyn-y-waun**', or 'John Jones, **Hafod-lon**'. The designation, once ascribed, would be a permanent one. Examples of such usage abound, and the practice of adding the house-name to that of the occupant is a continuing feature in most Welsh-speaking districts. Wales's greatest hymn writer is still formally referred to in this manner: William Williams, **Pantycelyn**.

Shop-names:

Local fairs and markets, together with itinerant packmen had hitherto played an important part in the social and domestic life of rural Wales. These, in their several ways supplied country dwellers with much of their basic requirements: utensils, cloth, foodstuffs, livestock . . . By the middle of the nineteenth century, as in England, their frequency and influence had begun to wane. One of the reasons for this may be traced back to the steady growth in the numbers of small shops. Evidence exists of a group of related names apportioned to buildings stemming from this phenomenon. The names were not in themselves

Welsh but were very much part of the scene at that time and remained so for the first decades of the twentieth century. These were the shop-names fashionable in the towns and villages. They also demonstrate the pervasive influence of the English language on the world of commerce in Wales during the period. Nevertheless, at the time, the shops performed a social as well as an economic function and were, together with the chapel and the tavern, the main centres of community life providing a point of contact and a ready source of news and information for the inhabitants of the locality. Local merchants, whose premises were labelled: **London House, Liverpool House, Manchester House, Bristol House, Sheffield House, Bradford House, Melbourne House, Dresden House, Paris House, Boston house . . .** strove thereby to impress upon their customers that the goods on display were somehow connected directly with warehouse stocks and current fashions prevailing in those great afore-mentioned ports and cities far beyond Offa's Dyke. In addition, there would have been several establishments bearing grander titles and many with connotations even further afield. They were: **The Emporium, The Exchange, Empire Stores, American Stores, Hong Kong Stores, Pretoria Stores, Lisbon Stores, Soho Stores, Victoria Stores, Regent Stores, Royal Stores, Crown Stores, Cambrian Stores, Gwalia Stores, Bon Marché . . .** and whose merchandise ranged from pin-cushions and petticoats to paraffin and partridges. These were the small-scale, commercial business enterprises of the day, the precursors of later departmental stores and the forerunners of the supermarket and hypermarket era. There was however one significant difference between them and today's multinationals. With few exceptions, each was financed and managed by its owner, who usually supervised and scrutinised all the intricate proceedings involved in 'buying and selling'. Some of the owners lived above, behind or below the premises and enjoyed the additional prestige that those establishments gave to their titles, as in, 'Mr Islwyn Rogers, **London House**', or 'David Davies, Esq., **Paris House**'.

Historical occasions and house-names:

Welshmen in considerable numbers have fought bravely in battle, and many have died 'for king and country' from the time of Henry VII onwards. They would have enlisted in a variety of regiments in the British Army, or manned the decks of countless ships of the Royal Navy. Their exploits on land and sea would have been followed with intense interest by family and friends, and particular historic occasions would have been enduringly commemorated, in Wales as well as in England, by such novel house-names as: **Balaclava House, Mafekin House, Minden House, Trafalgar House, Waterloo House . . .**[9]

Fashionable house-names:

There is no evidence among Welsh house-names of the influence of current, trendy English house-names, such as **Cobwebs, Hisaners, Itzmyne, Jusferus, Linga Longa, Luksier, Popinagen, Sootsus, Warra Norra . . .**[10] Neither is there any obvious attempt to emulate the practice sometimes observed in England, and mischievously used by Dylan Thomas in *Under Milk Wood* in his coining of 'Llareggub', where the order of the letters of an original name or phrase is reversed and the subsequent composition affixed to the dwelling as in **Sivam** from Mavis, **Retlaw** from Walter, **Arod** from Dora, **Rovert** from Trevor . . . There are however a few examples of more recent origin that tend to reflect a more pragmatic attitude towards modern-day living: **Dim-ar-ôl, Dros-dro, O'r diwedd, Dyma-ni, Seibiant, Ymdrech** . . . One popular Welsh actor and entertainer has named his Cardiff home **Drws-Nesa**.[11]

Welsh house-names – a major difference:

There seems to be nevertheless a significant difference in the way in which the Welsh as a people separate the sacred from the secular, in as much as house-names are concerned. In England, there are copious examples of house-names that follow the pattern: **St John's House, St James's Villa, St Margaret's, St Julia's Cottage, St Peter's Lodge, St Stephen's** . . . These names are not replicated as Welsh house-names and their counterpart in Welsh does not exist. In Spain, it is customary to dedicate each house in the name of one of the country's myriad saints.[12] A similar tradition prevails in Portugal. That there is an utter absence of such usage in Wales is probably due to the strong residual influence of Puritan radicalism that may be traced as far back as the mid-seventeenth century. Even so, Welsh house-names with some religious connotations do exist, but only in so much as they refer to the houses of the clergy (ordained ministers of religion in the Established or Nonconformist Churches). These are: **Y Ficerdy, Y Mans, Persondy, Llety'r Bugail, Llys Esgob, Plas Esgob, Canondy, Rheithordy, Tŷ'r Capel** but not **Tŷ Cwrdd**.[13] The names **Gwynfa** and **Paradwys** do not infringe upon any religious parameters but declare along with **Bodlondeb** and **Noddfa**[14] some of the most joyous attributes of 'home'.

A house by any other name . . .

With the passage of time, some Welsh place-names, along with many Welsh house-names have changed their form. The nature of these changes and the influences which have caused such changes over the years are the subject of linguistic and historical research. Frequently, a corrupted form will have supplanted the initial version and will have become mistakenly accepted as the original name. Consequently when an attempt is made to explain the meaning of that name the error may be considerable.

The Welsh house-name **Coedymwstwr**, rendered by some as 'whispering trees', illustrates the kind of misinterpretation that may occur when the present name is compared with its earlier form. As it stands in its present guise, the Welsh elements comprising the name are: *coed+y+mwstwr*. Professor Gwynedd O. Pierce comments:

> 'it is a good example of judgement based on the present form of the name, the Welsh dictionary definition of *mwstwr* 'noise, bustle' (a borrowing from English) being suitably adapted to apply to leafy surroundings . . .

The name is, indeed, attested in sixteenth century documentation but the implications of its true meaning take us back to the period of pre-Norman, probably earlier Christian settlements in Wales and is therefore of great significance.

On the basis of comparative evidence which is gradually emerging it appears that the original form of what is now *mwstwr* was *mystwyr*, and that this was ultimately a borrowing from Latin *monasterium* 'monastery'. The Latin form is the basis of English *minster*, French *moutier*, Breton *moustoer*, Irish *mainister* etc . . .

In the case of **Coedymwstwr** it may well be significant that the parish church of Coychurch, itself nearby was very probably the pre-Norman foundation of Llangrallo, where the remains of two tenth to early eleventh century crosses have been recorded.'[15]

Thus the name **coedymystwyr** would be translated 'trees of the monastery'.

Llety-tegan in the village of Rhydargaeau near the town of Carmarthen, exemplifies again the change that may occur to a house-name with the passage of time. Documentary evidence as far back as 1622 records the sale of **Lle ty Ieuan Deggan** (previously known as **Gilfach Gorrwg**), and subsequently as **Llety Deggan** (Deggan's dwelling). Usage and ignorance are responsible for the present version: **Llety-tegan** (Toy's dwelling).

The jocular comment quoted by Sir Ifor Williams in his book *Enwau Lleoedd:* 'Only fools would try to explain place-names!'[16] applies equally well to those who would attempt to explain house-names.

Welsh public house-names:

The descriptive house-name **Hendafarn** is far more explicit than **Y Llwyn**[17] or **Llwyndafydd** in revealing its former designation as a hostelry or tavern. Yet at some time or other each of the three buildings could well have been the setting where the weary traveller would have stopped awhile for refreshment and shelter. Throughout the ages such hostelries have been associated with travelling and with pilgrims particularly as the earliest class of travellers. Many of the taverns were originally sited on the pilgrim ways that led to the holy shrines. Their influence may still be seen, even today, in the south west corner of Pembrokeshire on roads leading to St David's Cathedral:[18] **The Grove, St Non's, The Old Cross** . . . and in North Wales on the Llŷn Peninsula on routes to Bardsey Island: **Y Gegin Fawr, Tu hwnt i'r afon, Sant Beuno** . . . At first, most of the taverns and inns of rural Wales were just ordinary houses or smallholders' cottages that opened their doors so that all and sundry might enter therein and have 'a bite to eat and a drop to drink'. In several villages and small towns in Wales, the tavern is still the building nearest the church and is usually located next to the churchyard gate. Frequently in the past, when a tavern had been established conveniently near a crossroads, bridge or ford, it would, with time, attract a cluster of houses, a smithy and possibly a small shop. The nucleus of a new village would have been formed, and on occasions it would take its name from that of the tavern,[19] as in: **Cross Inn, Cross Hands, Cross Foxes,**[20] **New Inn, Synod Inn** . . . In some instances, by today, the original tavern has long since closed its doors but its name lives on, in that of the village.[21]

Welsh house-names and Welsh hymn-tunes:

A cursory glance at the index pages of tunes in any Welsh hymnbook, such as: *Y Caniedydd, Caniedydd yr Ifanc, Emynau'r Eglwys, Llyfr Emynau a Thonau, Y Llawlyfr Moliant, Caneuon Ffydd* . . . immediately reveals a wealth of names currently in vogue as Welsh house-names. Examples abound: **Arfryn** composed by W. J. Evans (1866-1947); **Berwyn** composed by Caradog Roberts (1878-1935); **Bryn-teg** composed by J. Ambrose Lloyd (1815-74); **Dan-y-graig** composed by D. Afan Thomas (1881-1928); **Derwen-las** composed by Haydn Morris (1891-1965); **Llanfair** composed by Robert Williams (1781-1821) . . . There has been however, no attempt in this work to examine the possible connection between Welsh house-names and the names of certain Welsh hymn-tunes. Such a study would undoubtedly prove to be both fruitful and fascinating.

'I name this house . . .'

The aptness of most Welsh house-names seemingly reflects the care and consideration which generations of former householders have given to the task of naming their properties.

Position, location, size, history, connections . . . were all factors and played their part in influencing the outcome.

There is the apocryphal story of a non-Welsh speaker who recently arrived in Wales and who moved into a new house. It was believed that the addition of a Welsh house-name would complement the property, and in next to no time a brightly painted name-plate appeared prominently displayed on the front porch.

Passers-by noticed the 'plaque' and politely knocked on the door in order to gain entry. Some commented upon the pleasant views, front and rear. Others judged the position of the fireplace and the adequacy of the headroom. One was even heard to declare that the house was 'airy and tastefully decorated'! The hapless, new owner suffered all stoically, believing that perhaps it was a quaint form of welcoming, a custom peculiar among the natives.

It was only later, when another of the unheralded and uninvited guests inquired about the 'asking price' that all was revealed. The impetuosity of the owner in adopting an instant Welsh house-name was solely to blame. Names such as: **Arfryn, Ardro, Ardwyn, Arberth, Arwel, Ar-ael, Arfron** . . . were seen as short and distinctive, but the discriminating householder, spoiled for choice, had unwittingly seized upon **Ar werth – FOR SALE!** Caution should be urged concerning these matters!

Signs of the times:

With the continuing spread of urbanisation and the increasing practice of numbering houses, coupled with the 'double glazing syndrome' involving front door and fanlight replacements, many Welsh communities have been or are being robbed of a unique feature of their individuality. Colourful and intriguing names have been displaced by cold characterless digits. However, not all property owners have wholly succumbed to the regimentation of numbers. A few have resorted to the written form, as in: **Seventeen, Fifty-six . . .** Originality is universally recognisable, for example: **Numba tw.** Of Wales's 1.2 million dwellings, only a small proportion carry Welsh house-names. When current electoral rolls, compiled by Local Authorities, are compared with those of forty or fifty years ago, the decline in use of Welsh house-names as an essential component in the addresses of today's electorate becomes very apparent.

Welsh house-names and the future:

Welsh house-names remain a fascinating feature of our heritage fuelling our imagination and curiosity regarding the former occupants who first named those early dwellings and whose descendents may still inhabit many of them today. Embedded in this collection of house-names is a fundamental question: 'What, in the first place, caused or motivated each of those house owners to assign a particular name to a particular house?' One obvious reason was that the owner required to identify his house by name from other properties in the same area in order that it could be clearly and readily located. Answers were sought from owner-occupiers who had inherited dwellings that had remained within the ownership of their families for generations. Frequently their relatives could recall and relate how or why an ancestor had chosen a specific name: **Colomendy, Drws-y-coed, Henllys, Penfro** . . . Explanations were forthcoming from owners living in more recently built houses for their reasons for devising their own house-names: **Am-nawr, Bod-feddyg, Dros-dro, Glynwen, O'r diwedd, Tŷ Ni, Ymdrech** . . . Little prompting was needed to unravel how several houses acquired such names as: **Ar-dro, Dan-y-castell, Ger-y-lli, Glanyrafon, Pen-y-bryn, Tŷ-canol, Tŷ Capel, Tŷ-gwyn, Tŷ-cornel** . . . There remained however a considerable number of house-names without any adequate supporting explanation and the compiler was left to ponder, speculate and formulate some of the possible reasons.

Fortunately, most of the Welsh house-names referred to in this collection may still be observed in various parts of Wales, the Border Counties, Cumbria, Cornwall, London's Sussex Gardens and as far afield as North America and Argentina.[22] Some of them will have to be rescued from obscurity, or require a little renovation. If more householders could be inspired to bestow Welsh names on their properties, names that may reflect their own place of origin, allude to the building's history, idealise the home or lyrically portray the dwelling in its setting, then local people, in addition to visitors, would have constant, meaningful reminders that Wales has not only a treasured heritage but also a separate identity.

REFERENCES

1. R. J. Thomas, *Afonydd a Nentydd Cymru*. Cardiff: University of Wales Press, 1938.
2. *MINERS' JOURNAL*. No. 16, Saturday 11th April, 1857, Pottsville, Pennsylvania.
3. See Alan Conway's short article: 'Welsh Emigration in the nineteenth century' in A. H. Roderick (ed.) *Wales through the Ages – Modern Wales*. Vol. II. Llandybïe: Christopher Davies (Publishers) Ltd., 1965.

   On the other side of the Altantic, in the U.S.A., new townships had sprung up with such names as **Bangor, Lampeter, Swansea, Wales . . .** Many of the Welsh immigrants had taken their native place-names with them as linguistic mementoes of their homeland and had planted them proudly in the rich soil of the New World.
4. R. Bryn Williams, *Y Wladfa*. Cardiff: University of Wales Press, 1962.
5. In Brittany, distinctively different from the rest of France, where the ubiquitous cobalt blue enamel house-number prevails, house-names do occur. Many look familiar: **Ty Maria, Ty Gabriel, Ty Mamm, Ty Glas . . .**
6. Eurwyn William, *Home-made Houses*. Dwellings of the rural poor in Wales. Cardiff: National Museum of Wales, 1988, pp. 5-6.
7. The most popular house-names in the United Kingdom are: **The Cottage, Rose Cottage, The Bungalow, The Coach House . . .** See *Halifax House-Name Survey* . . . October 2003 – 'The UK's Top 50 House-Names' – Halifax Building Society, Halifax, West Yorkshire. The Survey was compiled from the address details of 2.5 million Halifax mortgage accounts.
8. T. J. Morgan and Prys Morgan, *Welsh Surnames*. Cardiff: University of Wales Press, 1985.
9. **Jubilee House** is a typical house-name commemorating an historic occasion, far from the cry of battle.
10. **Cobwebs** may well be the acronym formed from 'Currently owned by West of England Building Society'. **Litomith,** another house-name found in England is similarly formed from 'Love is the only master in this house'.

11. Mr Dewi (Pws) Morris. *Source*: Mrs Ray Morris, Treboeth, Swansea. Also seen lately on Holy Island, off the coast of Northumberland, a dwelling adjoining the Lindisfarne Heritage Centre bearing the house-name: **Next door**.
12. House-names in Spain include **Casa Santa Isabella, Casa San Pablo, Casa Santa Margarita** . . . On the Costa Brava however, there are a few examples that are foreign to the local tradition: **Dunroamin, Costalot, Avarest, Popova, Ishy Inn** . . . None of the natives shelters behind these house-names.
13. **Tŷ Cwrdd** is the alternative name reserved by Welsh Nonconformists for **Y Capel** (The Chapel), the building where Christians meet together regularly to worship and hear the proclamation of the Good News.
14. **Noddfa** also appears as a chapel-name: **Capel Noddfa, Capel Dinas Noddfa** . . . In a survey of Welsh Congregational Chapels, the three most popular names were: **Capel Ebeneser, Capel Seion** and **Capel y Tabernacl**. Source: *Y Tyst*, 15th October, 1992.
15. *Western Mail*, 14th July, 1989. Letter to the Editor.
16. The words are those of another erudite scholar: Sir John Morris-Jones.
17. Evergreen bushes or branches of grapes have served as the traditional signs found hanging outside taverns and inns since Roman times. Names such as **The Bush Hotel, The Ivy Bush Inn, The Holly Bush Inn, Y Llwyn, Llwyndafydd** . . . still survive. The old proverb, 'Good wine needs no bush', refers particularly to this time honoured practice.
18. Throughout the centuries St David's has been a focal point for pilgrims. Two pilgrimages to St David's were considered by the faithful to equal one pilgrimage to Rome, whereas three were equivalent to one pilgrimage to Jerusalem.
19. In much the same manner, many a Welsh village is named after a particular Welsh chapel built in that location, as in the case of: **Bethel, Bethlehem, Beulah, Carmel, Gibeon, Hebron, Hermon, Nasareth, Nebo, Peniel, Saron, Salem** . . .
20. In some cases the names **Cross House, Tŷ Croes, The Cross** . . . may stem from the old custom of erecting wayside crosses to

comfort and succour travellers on their journeying. In Catholic countries, such as Spain and Portugal, small shrines can still be seen alongside many of their roads. Brittany is well renowned for its wayside 'Calvaries'.

21. For a fuller account of Welsh tavern-names see Myrddin ap Dafydd, *Enwau Tafarnau Cymru*, Llyfrau Llafar Gwlad, No. 9, Carreg Gwalch Press; Capel Garmon, 1988.
22. Though some 8,000 miles away, house-names in Patagonia include **Tŷ Nain, Tŷ Nest, Plas y coed, Tŷ'r Gaiman, Hendre, Drofa Dulog, Treorci, Bryn Gwyn, Bryn Crwn . . .** Source: *Cadwyn Cyd*. No. 11. February 1993.

LIST OF
WELSH HOUSE-NAMES

A

Aber-craf (Confluence of the River Craf).
This is an example of a place-name transferred as a house-name due to some personal ties of the householders with the village of Aber-craf, Powys where the River Craf rushes over a sparkling waterfall to join the River Tawe as it winds its way through the Swansea Valley to the sea.
Related house-names:
Aberdaron (Estuary of the river Daron).
A place-name transferred as a house-name. There is possibly a link between the occupant, past or present, and the village or parish of Aberdaron, North West Wales.
Aber-nant (Estuary of a brook/stream).
A place-name transferred as a house-name, due probably to the close connection of the householder with Aber-nant, a village and parish in Carmarthenshire, or a village near Aberdâr, in the County Borough of Rhondda Cynon Taf.
Abertawe (Estuary of the River Tawe – Swansea).
A place-name transferred as a house-name. It is perhaps a linguistic souvenir brought by the householder from the former Town and Port in South Wales, which is, by today a thriving City and County.

Aberth (Sacrifice).
The householders openly admit that possession of one's own home is seldom achieved without considerable sacrifice. *See*: **Ymdrech**.

Adar-y-nos (Birds of the night; Night birds).
This is not an aviary but here is an implied confession. The occupants of the dwelling are as industrious during the hours

of darkness as are their counterparts in the community during the daylight. Night owls are go-getters!

Ad-astra (*Latin*: To the stars).
The house-name expresses what home means to the occupants. The Latin motto of the Royal Air Force: *Per ardua ad astra*, 'Through difficulties to the stars', sums up succinctly the situation. This home is tangible evidence that the householders have successfully overcome the struggles and setbacks of earlier times.

Aelwyd, Yr (The hearth: the home).
Hearth and home are considered as one in this house-name. It is where the fireplace stood, the cooking accomplished, the family congregated and the comforts of home were savoured.

Ael-y-bryn (Brow of the hill).
In this descriptive house-name, the position of the dwelling, on or near the brow of the hill, is significant.
   Related house-name:
Ael-y-don (Edge of the wave).

Aeron (River Aeron; berries).
A river's name is transferred as a house-name and identifies the occupant with a particular location. Also, the house may be surrounded by berry-bearing bushes or trees and as such may account for the name.

Aethnen (Aspen, trembling poplar).
The location of this shimmering tree, at or near the dwelling is the significant feature adapted by the occupants

as their house-name. *See*: **Afallen-deg, Bryn-Myrtwydd, Celyn, Derwen** . . .

Afallen-deg (Beautiful apple tree).
The house-name stems from a feature close to the dwelling itself. An apple tree in blossom has a charm of its own. In autumn its fruit is very acceptable.

Afallon (The enchanted isle in the west, to which Arthur was borne when wounded in battle).
This house-name recalls part of the fifth century Arthurian legend, the greatest contribution of the Celts to world literature.

Ail-dro (Second time).
The name may refer to some second occasion, perhaps a second attempt at setting up home in a different area.
   Related house-names:
Ail-gartref (Second home).
Ail-gynnig (Second chance; Second try).
Ail-le (Second place).

Allt-dderw (Oak wood; oak hill).
From this descriptive house-name, it is clear that the dwelling is situated close to oak-trees or is encompassed by them. A hill may also feature in the neighbourhood.
   Related house-names:
Allt-ddu (Black wood; black hill).
Allt-fach (Little hill; little wood).
Allt-fawr (Big hill or wood).
This is the name of a mountain near Ffestiniog, Gwynedd possibly transferred as a house-name.

Allt-fedw (Birch hill or wood).
Allt-frân-ddu (Black-crow's hill or wood).
Allt-gerrig (Hill of stones).
Allt-goch (Red hill or red wood).
Allt-lwyd (Grey hill or wood).
Allt-uchaf (Highest wood or hill).
Allt-wen, Yr (The white hill).

A place-name transferred as a house-name perhaps due to close ties between the occupant and the village of Yr Alltwen, Pontardawe in the Swansea Valley.

Allt-y-cadno (The fox's hill or wood).
Allt-y-ffynnon (Hill of the fountain).
Allt-y-gog (The cuckoo's wood).
Allt-y-grug (The heather hill).

This is a place-name transferred as a house-name. It is used by the occupant probably to display his affinity for Allt-y-grug mountain near Ystalyfera in the Swansea Valley.

Allt-y-maes (The field's hill or wood).
Allt-y-mynach (The monk's hill or wood).
Allt-y-perchyll (The piglets' hill).
Allt-yr-eryr (The eagle's hill or wood).
Allt-yr-hendre (Hill or wood of the old home).
Allt-yr-odyn (The lime-kiln hill).
Allt-yr-ynn (The ash grove or wood; Hillside of the ash trees).

A descriptive place-name in Newport has possibly been transferred as a house-name.

Allt-y-werin (The people's hill or wood).
Allt-y-wern (The alder-wood hillside).
Allt-y-wiber (The viper's grove or hill).
Allt-y-widdon (The witch's hill, The witch's wood).

Almeriana (A registered ship's name).
This is a ship's name transferred as a house-name. When the master of the vessel retired from the sea he may well have brought with him the ship's name as a souvenir of his maritime days and affixed it to his new abode in one of the coastal towns or ports of Wales.
Related house-name:
Almora (A registered ship's name).

Am-nawr (For now).
A house-name that is short and to the point. 'This-will-do-for-now,' a temporary residence perhaps until the boat comes in, or until the policy matures, or the crock of gold is discovered at the rainbow's end, or . . . The name offers a little hope and requires much faith.
Related house-name:
Amysbaid (For a while).

Angorfa (Anchorage; Harbour).
Here is a house-name that extols the virtues of home. This is the place where the worker, the traveller, the son, the daughter . . . may drop anchor at the end of the day. It is the safe harbour in all of life's storms, and regenerates one for the new day.

Anheddfa (Abode).
The house-name proclaims that the dwelling is a place in which the residents exist and live. It is wholly and simply a home.
Related house-names:
Anheddle (Dwelling place).
Annedd (Dwelling place).

Annedd-wen (Blessed dwelling place; White dwelling place).

Annwyl-fan (Cherished place).
This house-name reveals what home means to many: a dear place, a blessed place where joy and happiness are shared with the family.

Ar-ael (On a brow or ridge).
The descriptive house-name locates this dwelling immediately. Its position is pin-pointed on the brow of a hill.
Related house-names:
Arafon (Close by a river).
Arallt (On a hill; On a wooded hill).
Ar-bwys (Near or close to).
Ar-ddôl (On a meadow).
Ardwyn (On a hillock).
Ar-fin-y-môr (On the seashore, at the seaside).
Arfron (On a hillside).
Arfryn (On a hill).
Argel (A retreat; A refuge).
Aspects of the ideal home are reflected in this house-name. The comfort, the quietness, the reassurance, the seclusion, the privacy . . . are some of the attributes of such a place when day is done.
Argoed (By a wood).
The house-name could also have been transferred from the place-name Argoed, a village near Bedwellte, Monmouthshire.
Argraig (On a rock).
Arhosfa (A dwelling place, a stopping/resting-place).

Ar-lan (On a shore).
Ar-lan-y-môr (On the seashore).
Arlechwedd (On a hillside).
Arlyn (On a lakeside).
Arwerydd (By or beside an ocean).
Ar-y-bryn (On the hill).
Ar-y-glyn (On the glen).

Awel-deg (Beautiful breeze).
The breeze that freshens and invigorates is beautiful. A location away from city stife and industrial pollution where such a fresh breeze blows is the place to dwell. The dweller rejoices in the house-name.
   Related house-names:
Awel-dyner (Gentle breeze).
Awelon (Breezes).
Awel-y-ddôl (The meadow breeze).
Awel-y-don (The wave's breeze).
Awel-y-môr (The sea breeze).
Awel-y-mynydd (The mountain breeze).

B

Babell, Y (The tent or pavilion).
This house-name harks back to the time when dwellings were of a more temporary nature: moveable and portable shelters, perhaps supported by poles. Such dwellings continue to be a feature of the nomadic Bedouins' way of life in the Middle East. Also the place-name of the village near Ysgeifiog, Flintshire, may have been transferred as a house-name due to the personal ties of the householders with that location.

Banc-gelli-las (Greenwood hill).
This descriptive house-name conjures up a rural scene – a hillside of flourishing trees. The dwelling is either on part of that hillside or close to it.
Related house-names:
Bancyfelin (The mill hill).
Also, the place-name of the village near St. Clears (Sanclêr), Carmarthenshire, may have been transferred as the house-name due to the occupants' close connections with the village.
Banc-yr-eithin (The gorse hill).

Banwen (The moorland of cotton-grass).
The place-name of the locality near Onllwyn and Seven Sisters in the County Borough of Neath Port Talbot, has been transferred as a house-name, in all probability because the dwelling's occupants hail from that particular area.

Beili-bychan (Small yard or enclosure).
An attribute of the dwelling is emphasised in this descriptive house-name. It possesses a relatively small yard or enclosure.
Related house-name:
Beili-mawr (Big yard or enclosure).

Berllan bêr (Luscious orchard).
In this descriptive house-name reference may be made to the very location of the dwelling, within this fruitful orchard. It could be a pleasant view from the dwelling.
Related house-names:
Berllan dawel (Peaceful orchard).
Berllan deg (The fine orchard).

Berllan dywyll (Dark orchard).
Berllan, Y (The orchard).

Berth-ddu (Black bush or hedge).
Some properties are notable for their hedges. This dwelling may be bounded by such a feature. The descriptive house-name may refer to a single bush strategically placed in front or beside the dwelling.
   Related house-name:
Berth-lwyd (Brown or grey bush or hedge).
Also, the place-name of a locality near Gowerton (Tregŵyr), County of Swansea, may have been transferred as a house-name for personal reasons.

Berwyn, Y (The white summit).
This house-name has been happily transferred from the name of the mountain in Denbighshire. Doubtless the views of the mountain remain in the memory of the occupant.

Betws (House of prayer: A birch grove).
This house-name has been transferred from a village and parish place-name in Carmarthenshire or a parish place-name in Monmouthshire. 'Betws' occurs as an element in many place-names in Wales: Betws Bledrws, Betws Cedewain, Betws Garmon, Betws-y-Coed . . .

Beudynewydd (New cowshed).
A straightforward descriptive house-name. It proclaims the earlier pedigree of the building. The recycling of barns, railway stations, churches, chapels, schools . . . as

habitable dwellings is at present seen as profitable and fashionable.

Blaenau (Uplands or remotest region).
Here is an example of a place-name transferred as a house-name. The occupants of the dwelling may have had close ties with the town of Blaenau, Aberystruth, Monmouthshire.
Related house-names:
Blaen-cwm (Upper reaches of a valley).
This house-name is transferred from the place-name of the village of Blaen-cwm in the County Borough of Rhondda Cynon Taf.
Blaen-gwawr (First light of dawn).
Also, it can well be a house-name transferred from the place-name of the locality near Aberdâr in the County Borough of Rhondda Cynon Taf.
Blaen-nant-yr-hebog (Upper reaches of the falcon's brook).
Blaen-sawdde (Source or upper reaches of the River Sawdde).
This is also the uphill region – the source of the Sawdde, a tributary of the River Tywi, Carmarthenshire.
Blaen-waun (Upper reaches of moorland).
This place-name, a locality, near Llandisiliogogo, Ceredigion, has been transferred as a house-name.
Blaen-y-berllan (Front of the orchard).

Blawty (Meal or flour-house).
With this descriptive house-name the former use of the building is recalled. The dwelling is the richer for its past history and the occupants are proud of the association.

Blewyn-glas (Blade of green grass).
An allusion possibly to the rural location of the dwelling – set amongst verdant pastures and encompassed by peace and tranquillity.

Blodeufa (Flower garden).
The dwelling bearing this descriptive house-name stands surrounded by a beautiful garden of colourful flowers. With careful planning and diligence by the occupants a succession of blooms can be maintained throughout the four seasons: snowdrop, crocus, jasmine, tulip, daffodil . . .

Bod Alwyn (Alwyn's residence).
This dwelling is not to be confused with any other. The descriptive house-name declares that Alwyn dwells therein (or at an earlier period). Personal names do feature in some house-names.
Related house-names:
Bodawen (Home of the Muse).
Bod-feddyg (Doctor's residence).
Bod Ifor (Ifor's residence).

Bodlondeb (Contentment).
Joy of joys, here is a house-name that extols the virtues of the ideal home. Within the walls of this dwelling the occupants find satisfaction and fulfilment – a desirable property!

Brig-y-don (Crest of the wave).
From its house-name this dwelling is positioned near the coast. Land, sea and sky formulate the view. The idyllic

scene contains the cry of the gull, the crest of the wave and the crash of the breaker.
Related house-name:
Brig-y-nos (Late evening, nightfall).

Brodawel (Quiet vale or region).
Situation features in this descriptive house-name. The neighbourhood, the area, the spot itself is peaceful and pleasant. This is an ideal place in which to live. The dwelling is well placed and the occupants fortunate.
Related house-names:
Brodirion (Gentle vale or region).
Bro-huan (Sun vale).
Bro-Nest (Nest's vale or region).
Bro Iona (Iona's vale or region).

Bronallt (Forest hill).
Two elements in the countryside are combined in this descriptive house-name. The dwelling is either perched on a wooded hillside or close to it.
Related house-names:
Bron-deg (Beautiful hillside).
Bronheulog (Sunny hillside).
Bronhyfryd (Beautiful hillside).
Bronnant (Brook's hillside).
Also, the place-name of a village in the parish of Lledrod Isaf, Ceredigion, could have been transferred as the house-name because of the occupants' personal connections with that village.
Bronwydd (Wooded hillside).
This is also the name of a village near Carmarthen and now transferred as a house-name.

Bron-y-coed (The forest hillside).
Bron-y-wawr (The dawn's hillside).

Broséliâwnd (The large, dense forest, and cradle of sorcery in sixth century Britanny, where Myrddin (Merlin) was endowed with much of his magical skills).
A place-name from the Celtic past, identified today with Paimpont Forest between Rennes and Plöermel in Brittany, and transferred as a house-name. This house offers rest, security and comfort to the dwellers who see virtue in reminding all of the rich heritage of Celtic literature.

Bro-werdd (Green vale).
A descriptive house-name that refers to the location of the dwelling. Wales as a land of song, hills and rain can also boast of its green lowlands. The occupants of this property see the meadows and pastures near their home. *See*: **Brodawel**.

Brychgoed (Mottled trees).
Trees, light and shade are the ingredients implied by this house-name. People are considerably influenced by their surroundings and in this instance the environment is praiseworthy. The occupants of the dwelling proclaim the beauty of the view.

Bryn, (Y) ((The) hill).
The dominating feature in the locality is the hill, and as such it figures naturally as the house-name. The dwelling itself is either built on it or has a commanding view of it. It could also be the place-name of a village near Llanelli, Carmarthenshire or that of a village near Port Talbot,

transferred as a house-name because of the occupants' affinities with one of those places.

Related house-names:

Bryn-Amlwg (Exposed hill; conspicuous hill).
On the other hand, the name of a mountain near Llanbrynmair, Powys and possibly transferred as the house-name.

Bryn-aur (Gold hill).

Bryn-awelon (Hill of breezes).

Bryn-bach (A little hill).

Bryn-banadl (Broom hill).

Bryn-bedw (Birch hill).

Bryncastell (Castle hill).

Brynceffylau (Horses' hill).

Bryncelyn (Holly hill).
Also the name of a village in Flintshire.

Bryn-cerdd (Hill of song).

Bryn-cerrig (Hill of stones).

Bryn-coch (Red hill).
This could also be the place-name of a village near Neath, South Wales, transferred as a house-name due to the dwellings' occupants' close connections with that village.

Bryn-coed (Wooded hill).

Bryn-deri (Oak hill).

Bryn-eglur (Distinct hill).

Bryneglwys (Church hill).
Also, the place-name of the village and parish in Denbighshire could have been transferred as a house-name due to the existence of close ties between the occupants and Bryneglwys.

Bryn-eithin (Gorse or furze hill).

Bryn-glas (Green hill).

Note: In Welsh *glas* may mean green or blue.

Bryn-gobaith (Hope hill).
Bryn-gwastad (Smooth hill).
Bryn-gwylan (Gull hill).
Bryngwyn (White, fair or blessed hill).
This is also the place-name of a locality in Llan-arth Fawr, Monmouthshire, or of a parish in Powys that may have been transferred as a house-name for personal reasons peculiar to the occupants.
Bryn-haf (Summer hill).
Bryn-hawddgar (Pleasant hill).
Brynhedydd (Lark hill).
Bryn-heli (Sea hill).
Bryn-helyg (Willow hill).
Brynheulog (Sunny hill).
Brynhyfryd (Beautiful hill).
Also, it may be the place-name of a locality near Swansea City, transferred as a house-name because the occupants are from that area or have some other connections with Brynhyfryd.
Bryn-lleian (Nun's hill).
Bryn-llwyd (Grey hill).
Bryn Llywelyn (Llywelyn's hill).
Bryn-march (Stallion's hill).
Bryn Mawr (Big hill).
Also, the place-name of three mountains, one in Denbighshire and two in Powys, of a town and parish in Powys, or a locality near Caernarfon, Gwynedd may have been transferred as a house-name due to the personal connections of the dwelling's occupants. The prestigious American University Bryn Mawr, is so named for precisely such a reason.
Bryn-mebyd (Childhood hill).

Bryn-mefus (Strawberry hill).
Brynsiencyn (Jenkin's hill).
This may be the place-name of a village near Llanidan, Anglesey, that has been transferred as a house-name because of the dwelling's occupants' close ties with that area.
Bryn-siriol (Pleasant hill).
Bryn-syfi (Strawberry hill).
See: **Bryn-mefus**.
Bryn-teg (Beautiful hill).
It could also be the place-name of a village at Broughton, Denbighshire, or at Llanfair Mathafara Eithaf, Anglesey, transferred as a house-name because of the personal ties between the dwelling's occupants and Bryn-teg.
Bryntirion (Gentle hill).
Bryn-ysgallog (Thistly hill).
Bryn-y-môr (The sea hill).
Bryn-y-castell (The castle hill).
Also the name of a mountain due north of Carno, Powys.
Brynypentref (The village hill).
Bryn-y-pîn (The pinewood hill).
Bryn-yr-odyn (The kiln hill).
Bryn-yr-ychain (The oxen's hill).
Bryn-y-wawr (The dawn's hill).

Bugeildy (Shepherd's hut).
The house-name may well refer to the former use of the building as a shepherd's hut or shelter. In the refurbishing that has occurred the original name has survived unchanged. Also, the place-name of the village and parish in Powys may have been transferred as a house-name because of the

personal connections of the dwelling's occupants with Bugeildy.
Related house-name:
Bugeilfa (Sheep-walk).

Bwlch-bach (Little pass).
This descriptive house-name refers to the mountain pass in the locality. The passage through the mountains in this particular case is relatively small. The dwelling is so situated with a fine view of this geographical feature.
Related house-names:
Bwlch Gwyn (White pass).
This probably is a direct transference of the place-name of the pass at Pentrefoelas, Conwy County Borough, or that of a village near Brymbo, Wrecsam County Borough, due to the dwellings' occupants' close ties with either of those areas.
Bwlch Mawr (Great pass).
The name of the mountain at Clynnog, Gwynedd, has probably been transferred as a house-name due to the personal connections of the dwelling's occupants with that region.
Bwlch-y-fedwen (The birch-tree gap).
Bwlch-y-ffin (The boundary gap).
Bwlch-y-gwynt (The wind's pass).

Bwthyn, (Y) ((The) cottage).
The name indicates the nature of the dwelling. It is not a house, a bungalow or a chalet. It is a cottage and by definition, small and possibly old.
Related house-names:
Bwthyn Blodwen (Blodwen's cottage).
Bwthyn cornel (Corner cottage).

Bwthyn-gwyn (White cottage).
Bwthyn-haul (Sun cottage).
Bwthyn-hedd (Peace cottage).
Bwthyn-llechog (Cottage of slates).
Bwthyn Mai (May's cottage).
Bwthyn Ni (Our cottage).
Bwthyn-pîn (Pine cabin).
Bwthyn-y-blodau (Cottage of the flowers).
Bwthyn-y-felin (The mill cottage).
Bwthyn-yr-enfys (The rainbow cottage).
Bwthyn-y-wawr (The dawn's cottage).

C

Cae-crwn (Round field).
The location of the dwelling is paramount in connection with this descriptive house-name. The house is set in a circular field and that in itself is sufficiently distinctive to warrant the name.

Related house-names:
Cae-ffair (Fair field).
Cae-glas (Green field).
Note: *glas* is the Welsh word for 'green' as well as 'blue'.
Cae-gwyn (White field).

Caer Arba (Arba's fort).
This unusual and remarkable house-name is Bible based. Arba was a giant of a man and the legendary founder of Hebron in Israel. His descendants were all tall men and it is reputed that they frightened Moses's scouts by their very size. (*See*: Genesis 35:27; Joshua 14:15; 15:13 . . . Obviously

the inhabitants of this dwelling required a house-name that would be significantly different from those of their neighbours.

Cae'r efail (Forge field).
The past use of the field where the present dwelling stands is referred to in this descriptive house-name. In earlier times the smithy was an important centre in every locality and the field would have held the horses to be shod and the carts to be repaired.
Related house-names:
Cae'r gof (The smith's field).
Cae'r gog (The cuckoo's field).
Cae'r gors (The field of the marsh).
Cae Rhys (Rhys's field).
Cae'r march (The stallion's field).
Cae'r odyn (Field of the kiln).
Cae'r wylan (The gull's field).
Cae'r ywen (Field of the yew tree).

Caledfryn (Rough or hard-to-climb hill).
This house-name describes the nature of the location. The dwelling is situated on a rough or steep gradient.

Cam-nesaf, Y (The next step).
With this house-name one is left in a quandary. What is the next step to be? An extension, a move to another place perhaps, or is this house-name the sole survivor of an earlier penultimate stage when the prospective householders tentatively approached the vacant building plot and proudly proposed their intention to build as 'Y cam nesaf'?

Canol-y-maes (Middle of the meadow).
This house-name clearly defines the dwelling's exact location: it stands in the middle of the meadow.

Cân-y-gwynt (The wind's song).
This house-name expresses lyrically the wind's contribution to the dwelling's location. It serenades beneath its windows and sings around its walls.
Related house-names:
Cân-y-gog (The cuckoo's song).
Cân-y-môr (The sea's song).
Can-y-nant (The stream's song).
Cân-yr-afon (The river's song).
Cân-yr-ehedydd (The lark's song).
Cân-yr-eos (The nightingale's song).

Carnau (Cairns).
The remarkable view is probably referred to in this descriptive house-name. A number of cairns or mounds of stones, possibly from the pre-Christian era, are visible from the dwelling.
Related house-names:
Carnedd (Cairn).
Carnglas (Blue cairn).
The dwelling may possibly be near a blue-stone cairn and this would account for its distinctive house-name. Also, the place name of a locality in Swansea, may have been transferred as a house-name because of family or social ties with that area.
Carnlwyd (Grey cairn).
Also, the place-name of a mountain near Morriston, Swansea, may have been transferred as a house-name due to the householders' ties with that locality.

Carn-y-bugail (The shepherd's cairn).
Carn-y-wiwer (The squirrel's cairn).
See: **Garn, Y**.

Carreg-lwyd (Grey rock).
The notable feature in the locality is the grey rock. It dominates the landscape and gives the dwelling's occupants an opportunity for an appropriate house-name.
   Related house-names:
Carreg wen (White stone or rock).
Carreg-y-felin (The millstone).

Cartref (Home, a dwelling place).
In this dwelling the occupant and his or her family usually reside. It is where each sets out from in the morning and returns to, at the end of the day. This is where souls are refreshed, family ties renewed and batteries recharged. Home is where individuals are encouraged to be themselves. **Cartref** is the most popular house-name in Wales.
   Related house-names:
Cartrefle (Homestead, abode).
Cartref Ni (Our home).
Cartrefol (Homely).
Cartref-tirion (Gracious home).

Castell-bach (Little castle).
The occupants of this dwelling see their home as a castle, albeit a small one. It is their stronghold and defence against the external world and its problems. The house-name expresses their attitude.
   Related house-names:
Castell-draenog (Hedgehog's castle).

Castell gwylan (Gull's castle).
Castell-y-cimwch (The lobster-pot).
Castell-y-geifr (The goats' castle).

Cefn Cadle (Battlefield ridge).
This is an example of a place-name that has been transferred as a house-name. The probability is that the dwelling's occupants maintain strong ties with the locality of Cefn Cadle, Fforestfach, Swansea.
Related house-names:
Cefncoed (Ridge of trees).
Cefn-fforest (Forest highland).
Cefnfor (Ocean).
Cefn-glas (Green ridge).

Cell Ifor (Ifor's cell).
In this descriptive house-name, Ifor's dwelling is compared with a hermit's cell, a retreat, a small enclosed place separate and distinct from the external world. It is what the occupants require from their home.

Celliwig (Hazel grove; Kellewik).
Part of our Celtic history is recalled by this house-name. It refers to a possible location of King Arthur's Court in Cornwall.

Celyn (Holly).
Trees figure frequently in Welsh house-names. In this example holly-trees feature as the main attraction with their shiny green leaves and blood red berries. The trees may surround the dwelling or grow close by.

Cerdd-y-don (The wave's song).
In the maritime location the sound of the sea is captured in this poetic house-name. Obviously the dwelling's occupants enjoy their closeness to the shore and to the sound of the ebb and flow of the tide.

Cerdinen (Rowan-tree).
Feather-like green foliage and orange-red berries of a nearby rowan-tree offer the occupants an irresistible house-name.

Cernyw (Cornwall).
Ties between the Welsh and Cornish people have always been close and firm. Both are Celts. Language, landscape, coastline . . . have many similarities. There is little wonder that this place-name has been transferred as a house-name. There may be a score of private reasons why the dwelling's occupants cherish the links between Wales and Cornwall. Long may they endure.

Cerrig-gleision (Blue stones).
The house-name probably describes the material from which the dwelling has been built. Blue stones may also refer to the rocks quarried from the Preseli Hills in Pembrokeshire and noted for their use by the Beaker People in their construction of Stonehenge during the Bronze Age around 2000 B.C.

Cesail-y-bryn (The hill's sheltered or secluded spot).
The dwelling's location is mentioned in the house-name. The building stands in a nook on the hill and is ideally situated.

Ceunant (Ravine).
The local terrain where the dwelling is situated features a ravine. This deep, mountain cleft is an aspect which the occupants wish to highlight in the house-name. The property obviously stands at a vantage point *vis-à-vis* the scenery.

Cileos (Nightingale's retreat).
The dwelling is situated where a nightingale's plaintive anthem may be heard. The meadows, hill-sides and valley-glades are charmed by the bird's nocturnal song. This descriptive house-name proclaims the occupants' delight.
   Related house-names:
Cilfach (Sheltered or secluded spot).
See: **Y Gilfach-glyd**.
Cil-haul (Sun's retreat; sun's sheltered place).
Ciloerwynt (Cold wind's retreat or nook).
Cilonnen (Ash-tree nook).
Cilrychen (Nook of the oxen).
Cilsant (Saint's retreat).
Cilwern (A nook near alder-trees).
Cil-y-cwm (River source of the valley).
This house-name is transferred from the place-name of the village and parish of Cil-y-cwm, Carmarthenshire. The dwelling's occupants probably have personal ties with that village or parish.

Clwydi-gwynion (White gates).
This property is to be recognised by its white gates. The dwelling's occupants have chosen a straightforward, no-nonsense name for the purpose. It functions well provided

that the neighbours are passionately fond of red, orange, green, blue, indigo, violet or black for *their* gates!

Clydfan (A warm and sheltered place).
This house-name describes the ideal site for a dwelling and contrasts with such house-names as: **Awelon, Bryn-awelon, Bwlch-y-gwynt, Crib-y-gwynt . . .**

Cnwc-y-barcud (The kite's hillock or knoll).
Situation is of prime importance in this house-name. The dwelling is on or near a hillock which is the favourite haunt of this large bird of prey. The rest of the location is left to the imagination.
Related house-names:
Cnwc-y-berllan (The orchard hillock).
Cnwc-y-bugail (The shepherd's knoll).
Cnwc-yr-eithin (The gorse knoll).
Cnwc-y-rhedyn (The fern knoll).

Coed-derw (Oak trees, oak forest).
The house-name describes a local feature, namely, a forest of mature oak-trees. The dwelling itself is in close proximity to the woods.
Related house-names:
Coed-duon (Blackwood).
Also a village in the County Borough of Caerphilly.
Coedfa (Woodland or forest).
Coedlan (Grove, woodland).
Coedlannau (Woodlands; *plural form of* **coedlan**).
Coed-mawr (Large forest).
Coedmor = Coed-mawr (Large forest).
Coed-mynach (Monk's wood).

Coedy-bach (Little dwelling in a wood).
Also, Coety is the place-name of a village and parish in the County Borough of Bridgend.
Coed-y-bryn (Trees of the hill).
Coed-y-cwm (Trees of the valley).
Coed-y-ffynnon (Grove of the spring).
Coed-y-gaer (Trees of the fort).
Coed-y-glyn (Trees of the glen or valley).
Coed-y-gof (The smith's trees).
Coed-y-llan (Trees of the church).
Coed-y-widdon (The witch's wood).

Colomendy (Dovecot).
All kinds of associations come to mind with this house-name. Is home likened to a dovecot where the fluttering of comings and goings are heard the daylong? Would a member of the family ever voice, 'O that I had wings like a dove; for then I would flee away'? In this dwelling the residents may be so devoted to one another that the resulting sounds are reminiscent of the cooing of turtle doves in a dovecot. Then again, there maybe just a dovecot on the premises.

Corlannau (Sheep-folds).
The pastoral view from the house is of many enclosures for penning sheep. The name is also that of an area near Port Talbot and may have been transferred from there as a house-name.
Related house-names:
Corlan-y-defaid (The sheepfold).
A traditional sheep-fold with its stone-walls and gate may be seen from the property. It is possible that the present

dwelling has been built on the site of a former sheep-fold. However, the occupants consider their home as a secure and refreshing place where all the family can congregate.
See: **Y Gorlan**.

Corn-yr-afr (Goat's horn).
This descriptive house-name may imply that the dwelling's occupants have an abiding interest in astrology and that Capricorn is their favourite sign of the zodiac. Also, it may simply be that a goat's horn was found there when the site was originally chosen as a location for the dwelling.

Craig-Ddu (Black rock).
This house-name relates to a black rock in the immediate vicinity. also the name of several cliffs/precipices in North Wales.
   Related house-names:
Craig wen (White rock).
Craig-y-don (Rock of the wave).
Craig-y-nos (Rock of the night).
An imaginative house-name that conjures up a night dark from pole to pole and shrouding a stark, sombre rock. (It was in such a setting that the celebrated Victorian opera singer Adelina Patti (1843-1919) set up home at **Craig-y-nos** in the upper reaches of the Swansea valley.)
Craig-y-drysni (Rock of the wilderness).
Craig-yr-allt (Rock of the hill).

Creigle (Rocky place).
There is no disillusionment connected with this descriptive house-name. The ground is stony and the site is rugged and

precipitous. Within the dwelling probably there is a warm, comforting ambience contrasting markedly with the external environment.

Crib-y-gwynt (Ridge of the wind, windy ridge).
Situation is paramount in this descriptive house-name. The mountain ridge referred to is the customary territory of the prevailing wind, and the dwelling's occupants are very aware of its blustery presence.

Cri'r Wylan (The gull's cry).
This house-name immediately suggests a maritime location. The dwelling's position is somewhere near the coast where the gulls screech and cry, and the taste of salt lingers in the moist air.

Croeso (Welcome, hospitality).
The Welsh are not merely a musical nation but a welcoming and hospitable one as well. This home declares its aim and objective plainly. The family returns gladly knowing that come what may within the four walls there will be an embracing, shared love for one and all on every occasion.

Cromlech (A dolmen).
Cromlechi (plural form of *Cromlech*) are the first substantial, permanent constructions of man. The earliest of these megalithic chamber-tombs from the Neolithic period, pre-date the first of the pyramids of Egypt by about fifteen hundred years. It is hardly likely that anyone has adapted one as a home! The probability is that there is a fine view of a *cromlech* from the dwelling itself.

Crud-y-gân (The song's cradle).
The poetic house-name reveals much concerning the dwelling's occupants. This is where singing is nurtured. All who reside here are music enthusiasts, soloists or choristers alike, and firm believers that it is the very 'food of love'.
Related house-names:
Crud-yr-awel (The breeze's cradle).
Crud-y-wawr (Cradle of the dawn).

Cuddfan (Hiding-place).
This house-name reveals one of the many facets of the ideal home. Here is a hiding place, a refuge from the busy, bustling world. It is where the soul is refreshed and vigour renewed for the next day.

Cwmcigfran (Raven's valley).
The dwelling, as the descriptive house-name implies, is located in a mountainous area. The valley referred to echoes to the harsh croaks of the raven.
Related house-names:
Cwm-clyd (Sheltered valley).
Cwmcoch (Red valley).
Cwm-Dwfn (Deep valley).
Cwm-eithin (Gorse valley).
Cwmffrwd (Swift-stream valley).
This is also the name of a district near the town of Carmarthen, possibly transferred as a house-name.
Cwm-heulog (Sunny valley).
Cwm-tawel (Quiet valley).
Cwm-tywyll (Dark valley).
Cwm-y-frân (The crow's valley).

Cwm-yr-aethnen (Valley of the aspen tree).
Cwm ysgyfarnog (Hare's valley).

Cwr-y-coed (Corner of the forest).
Situation governs the house-name in this example. The dwelling is built near the corner of the forest where flora, fauna, fur and feather flourish.

Cwrt-bach (Little mansion).
In this house-name home is seen as a mansion, albeit a small one. The delights and the benefits are to be shared by all the family.
Related house-names:
Cwrt-mawr (Grand mansion).
Cwrt-newydd (New mansion).

Cwts-bach (A small resting or hiding place).
A sense of security is implied by this descriptive house-name. A home, above all else, needs to be an acknowledged safe place of rest and revitalisation, away from the busy, booming world. The dwelling's occupants are well aware of such a necessity.

Cwyn-y-gwynt (The wind's lament).
Obviously the occupants of this dwelling speak of first-hand experience. The wind is a potent force to contend with, and its sound, moaning and groaning around the property, is an ever present reality. This descriptive house-names speaks volumes!

Cyfoeth-y-brenin (The king's riches/domain/subjects).
This house-name intrigues the observer. Are the riches

synonymous with the sphere of influence exercised by the Regent, or with the persons owing obedience to him? Also, it could be the straightforward transfer of a name found in the village of Llanfihangel Genau'r-glyn, Ceredigion.

Cynfelin (Former mill).
The present dwelling, bearing this house-name, either stands on the site of an earlier corn or woollen mill or is a modernised version of the original building retaining perhaps some of the old mill's more interesting features.

Cynghordy (Senate/meeting house).
The present dwelling may stand on the site of an earlier building used for the purpose of local government. Also, the home has always been an ideal location for members of the family to get together and discuss or advise. The place-name may have been transferred from Llanfair-ar-y-bryn, Carmarthenshire, and used as a house-name because of personal connections.

Cysgod-y-dderwen (The oak-tree's shadow).
This descriptive house-name locates the dwelling close to an oak-tree, which is the significant feature. In summer the house is shaded by its foliage and in winter the gnarled trunk and branches offer some protection from the blustery wind.
   Related house-names:
Cysgod-y-coed (The forest's shadow).
Cysgod-y-curyll (The hawk's shadow).
Cysgod-y-pinwydd (The pine-woods' shadow).
Cysgod-y-twˆr (The tower's shadow).

Cysondeb (Consistency).
With this house-name, the dwelling's occupants highlight one of the essential characteristics inherent in the ideal home, that is, the state of being consistent. Love, truth and faithfulness are the basis of family ties; standards are expected and maintained . . . Capriciousness, the very opposite, has no place on such a hearth.

D

Dantwyn (Below a knoll).
Location is evident in this straightforward, descriptive house-name. The dwelling itself has been built at the foot of some rising ground.
Related house-names:
Dan-y-capel (Below the chapel).
Dan-y-bryn (Below the hill).
Dan-y-castell (Below the castle).
Dan-y-coed (Below the woods).
Dan-(y)-deri (Below the oaks).
Dan-y-garreg (Below the stone).
Dan-y-graig (Below the rock).
The dwelling's occupants may hail from Dan-y-graig, near Yr Alltwen, in the Swansea Valley and have transferred the place-name as a house-name.
Dan-y-pentre (Below the village).
Dan-yr-allt (Below the hill or wood).
Dan-y-rhiw (Below the hill).
Dan-y-wenallt (Below the fair hill or wood).

Dawns-y-dail (Dance of the leaves).
This house-name stirs the imagination. The multi-coloured

leaves form the *corps de ballet* and the choreographer is the capricious autumn breeze. To the delight of the dwelling's occupants impromptu performances are observed throughout the day on selected sites!
   Related house-name:
Dawns-y-don (The wave's dance).

Defynnog (Possibly a personal name – son of Brychan (?)).
The place-name of the village near Maes-car, Powys, possibly transferred as a house-name because of some personal connections with the dwelling's occupants.

Degannwy (The town of the Decantae tribe).
A house-name formed by transferring the place-name of the village near Llan-rhos, Gwynedd. There is probably some close family connection that binds the two.

Deilen-wen (White leaf).
This descriptive house-name is eye-catching. Leaves are usually green, yellow or variegated, some might be russet-red or brown. The white willow is known for its silvery backed leaves. The dwelling's occupants have chosen a distinctive name for their property.

Delfan (Pretty place).
Here the indulgent householder has achieved his goal: windows sparkle, walls gleam, paths are weed free, flowers scent the air . . . this is an attractive place and adds to the concept of home.
   Related house-names:
Delfryd (An ideal).
Delfryn (Attractive hill).

Delyn Aur (Y) ((The) golden harp).
This is an unusual house-name. It is may be derived from the Welsh hymn-tune of that name. The words, usually sung to this tune are by William Williams, Pantycelyn (1717-1791). It remains a firm favourite in most Welsh Churches.

Deri (Oak-trees).
Situation governs the choice of house-name in this instance. The dwelling is located near an oak forest. This is also a place-name, that of a village near Gelli-gaer in the County Borough of Caerphilly.

Derlwyn (Oak grove, oak wood).
The oak trees referred to in the house-name are in close proximity to the dwelling. According to the occupants, they constitute a significant feature in the immediate vicinity. *See*: **Llwynderw**.
  Related house-names:
Derwen-aur (Golden oak).
This descriptive house-name may well refer to a variety of oak known as the Golden Oak of Cyprus – a small evergreen tree or shrub, first introduced to Britain in 1885.
Derwen-deg (Fair oak).
Derwen-Fach (Little oak).
Derwen-fawr (Large oak).
Also, it could be due to the transfer of the name of a locality in Swansea City, because of close connections between the occupants and that region.
Derwen-gam (Crooked oak).
Derwen-las (Green oak).
This particular name could well refer to the holm or holly

oak, which has evergreen leaves and may grow to a height of 25 to 27 metres, and which is a significant feature near the dwelling.
Derwydd (Oak trees).

Dihangfa (An escape).
With this unusual house-name, the occupants reveal an aspect of the ideal home. It is to be a place set apart from the drudgery of work, oppression and the other varied strictures that confine the individual. In the security of the home, matters are viewed differently, joy and peace prevail and dreams may be realised. This is the place to be.

Dim-ar-ôl (Nothing left).
With this amusing house-name, the householders declare unashamedly that the struggle involved in building or buying the 'desirable residence' has left them virtually penniless. Additional signs such as, 'No hawkers, pedlars, etc.' are unnecessary. The house-name tells it all!

Disgwylfa (Place of observation).
With this house-name, the occupants seek to enhance the concept of home. It is to be a watchful place where needs are assuaged and hopes fortified. Expectations grow and anticipation scents the air. Home is that place which pulsates with life and yet permits peace to linger and tranquillity to traverse its territory – a joyous domain.

Diwedd-yr-haf (End of the summer).
This unusual house-name may denote when the occupants first took up residence at the property. It could also refer to

the riot of colour, spectacular scenery and unrivalled views from the location at the close of each summer season.

Dolafallen (Apple-tree meadow).
This straightforward, descriptive house-name refers to the location of the dwelling. The property is either part of the meadow or in close proximity to it, enabling the occupants to share the idyllic scene.
Related house-names:
Dôl-afon (River meadow).
Dolau (Meadows, pasture).
Also, the name may have been transferred from that of the village Idole (**Y Dolau**), near Carmarthen because of close personal ties between the occupants and that place.
(*Note*: **Dolau** is the plural form of **dôl** – meadow, pasture, dale).
Dolaugwyrddion (Green meadows).
Dôl awel (Breeze's meadow).
Dôl-fêl (Honey meadow).
Dolfor (Big meadow).
Dôl-gam (Winding meadow).
Dôl-gerdd (Music meadow).
Dôl-gnau (Meadow of nuts).
Dôl-goch (Red meadow).
Dôl-Hafren (Meadow of River Severn).
Dôl-hardd (Beautiful meadow).
Dôl-huan (Sun meadow).
Dôl-wen (Fair meadow).
Also, the name may have been transferred from the village of Dôl-wen, near Betws-yn-Rhos, in the County Borough of Conwy, because of personal ties between the occupants and the village.

Dôl-werdd (Green meadow).
See: **Dolaugwyrddion**.
Dôl-y-bont (Meadow of the bridge).
Dôl-y-cadno (Meadow of the fox).
Dôl-y-coed (Meadow of the wood).
Dôl-y-felin (Meadow of the mill).
Dôl-y-gaer (Meadow of the fort).
Dôl-y-garreg-wen (Meadow of the white stone).
Dôl-yr-onnen (Meadow of the ash-tree).
Dôl-y-maen (Meadow of the stone or rock).
See: **Dôl-y-garreg-wen**.
Dôl-y-pandy (Meadow of the fulling-mill).

Drain-duon (Blackthorn).
This descriptive house-name probably refers to the blackthorn hedges enclosing the property. When cut and trimmed each Spring and Autumn they demonstrate the skill of the hedger and attract the admiration of many.

Dre-fach (Small homestead).
This is probably an example of a place-name transferred as a house-name. The dwelling's occupants may have close connections with, or hail from Dre-fach, a village near Newcastle Emlyn or one near Y Tymbl, both in Carmarthenshire, or from another near Llanwenog, Ceredigion.

Dros-dro (For a while).
Could this be a contemplative, philosophical house-name alluding to the impermanence of life in general and a warning to all and sundry that we are here, but for a while? On the other hand, the dwelling may be temporary accommodation until better becomes available.

Related house-names:
Dros-y-ddôl (Across the meadow).
Dros-y-ffordd (Across the way).
Dros-y-gors (Over the marsh).
Dros-yr-afon (Beyond the river).

Drws-y-coed (Opening in the woods).
The descriptive house-name refers to the dwelling's location. An appreciable gap in the woodlands is the cherished site for the dwelling. Also, the name may well have been transferred from the place-name of the locality near Llandwrog, Gwynedd.

Drysgoed (A thicket).
This house-name may well describe the prevailing condition of the site prior to the building of the property. It may have been a hard battle against nature and the householders remind everyone that originally it was arduous and difficult.
Related house-names:
Drysni (Thicket, wilderness).
Dryslwyn (A place full of brambles).
Also, it could well be the transference of the name of a locality or castle near Llangathan, Carmarthenshire due to some close connection between the dwelling's occupants and the original setting.

Dwrgi-bach (Little otter).
This house-name admits that there is a welcome visitor to the property. There must be a source of water, a river or stream, alongside the dwelling where the occupants may watch the playful otter perform.

Dychwelfa (A return, a recurrence).
This expressive house-name reveals an aspect of the ideal home. This is where the members of the family meet together and enjoy fellowship. It is the place from which they depart and return to, time and time again. This is the recurrence: the joy of living at home. The dwelling's occupants know it well.

Dyffryn (Vale or valley).
This house-name suggests that the dwelling is either situated in a valley or close by. The occupants have an uninterrupted view of the valley with a river or stream meandering through it. Also, the house-name may have been transferred from the place-name of a village near Llanenddwyn, Gwynedd; Llangynwyd, Bridgend County Borough; Merthyr Tudful or a parish in Monmouthshire. There may be close ties between the occupants and one of the places mentioned above.
Related house-names:
Dyffryn-aur (Gold(en) valley).
Dyffryn-braf (Pleasant valley).
Dyffryn-eos (Nightingale valley).
Dyffryn-golau (Light or bright valley).
Dyffryn-helyg (Valley of willow trees).
Dyffryn-teg (Beautiful valley).

Dyfnant (Ravine).
The dwelling bearing this house-name probably overlooks a deep, narrow gorge or mountain cleft. The spectacular scenery has a special fascination and the householders seize upon the phenomenon as their house-name.

Dyma-ni (Here we are).
A house-name that proclaims joyously that this is the dwelling, the residence that serves as home for all the family.
See: **Cartref**.

E

Ebrill (April–the fourth month of the year).
Is this house-name a constant reminder of Spring, gambolling lambs, the first cuckoo, primroses . . .? Is this the name of one of the occupants? Was this the appointed month when settlement displaced weary house-hunting, conveyancing and moving? One wonders.

Edmar (A composite form derived from **Ed**ward and **Mar**garet).
This house-name is a 'special edition' composed by the occupants themselves by combining parts of each other's names.

Efail, **Yr** (The smithy).
The building's former designation is recorded in the house-name. It tells of a past when anvils rang out, bellows billowed, horses were shod and times were different.
   Related house-names:
Efail-fach (Small smithy).
Also a place-name near the town of Neath.
Efailisaf (Lowest smithy).
Also a place-name near Llanilltud Faerdref, Pontypridd, possibly transferred as a house-name.
Efail-newydd (New smithy).
Also the name of a village near Pwllheli, Gwynedd.

Efail-wen (White smithy).
Also a place-name in South West Carmarthenshire.

Efo'r grug (With the heather).
This house-name indicates a rural location. The dwelling stands on heather-covered terrain surrounded by the purple colour of the moor or heath and far from the hustle and bustle of urban living. Follow the directions in order to find the householders!

Efrydfa (Study, place for meditation).
Home is a dwelling with many features. It can be a resting place. For the housewife it is frequently a work place. For the studious it may be *the* place to read, research and write. A home is greater than the sum of its parts.

Eglur (Clear, distinct, conspicuous, observable).
It could be that the view from the property is clear and not overshadowed by jutting rocks or overhanging cliffs. Then again the house-name could refer to the conspicuous location of the dwelling amidst green pastures or perhaps to its very position on the hillside.

Eiddil (A composite form derived from **Eidd**wen and **Ill**tud).
This house-name may be the result of combining part of the wife's name with part of the husband's, in order to fabricate a name for the property. (The Welsh adjective **eiddil** means weak, feeble, frail).

Ein cartref (Our house).
There is an emphatic air to this house-name. The householders

proudly proclaim, without fear or favour, that this is *their* home.
See: **Cartref** and **Tŷ ni**.

Eirianfa (Beautiful place).
This is a descriptive house-name that contributes to the concept of the ideal home. The occupants believe it to be desirable and beautiful both externally and internally. It is to them everything that home should be.

Ethin-aur (Golden gorse – *Ulex europaeus*).
The dwelling is situated in a part of the country where gorse or furze is a predominant feature of the landscape with its bright yellow flowers in bloom almost all the year round.
Related house-names:
Eithin duon (Black gorse).
Eithin gleision (Green gorse).

Elfelis (A composite form derived from **Elf**ed and **Elis**abeth).
Husband and wife combine to name their property with parts of their forenames. It is hoped that Fatima and Alan never get to naming their home in a similar manner!

Elusendy (Almshouse).
This house-name is an historic reminder relating to an earlier use of the building.

Encil (Retreat).
The house-name conveys one of the main aspects of home. It is to be a retreat from the pressures and strains of the working day. Here the busy world is hushed and the tempo

of living is reduced in order that a new dawn can again be faced with freshness and exuberance.

Related house-names:
Encil-y-coed (The forest retreat).
Encil-y-mynach (The monk's retreat).

Enfys (Rainbow).
Red, orange, yellow, green, blue, indigo and violet colours are all vividly obvious around the dwelling in flower and foliage. These householders are diligent gardeners. (*Enfys* is also a popular girl's name.)

Enlli (Bardsey Island).
Here is an example of a linguistic souvenir brought back by the occupants as a reminder of their visit to this idyllic island some two miles south west of the tip of Llŷn Peninsula. History would have it that 20,000 saints are buried there and that previously two pilgrimages to Enlli would be the equivalent of one to Rome, whereas three pilgrimages to the island would equal one to Jerusalem. Today, it remains uninhabited, offering a bird watcher's paradise in an area of legendary tranquillity.

Erddig (Small garden).
This house-name may well reflect the interest of the occupants in limited horticulture. It could also be the transfer of a parish-name in Denbighshire due to close family ties with that area.

Erw-deg (Fair acre).
The householders note that location, view and soil-quality are to their liking, hence the house-name.

Related house-names:
Erw-faethlon (Fertile acre).
Erw-galed (Hard acre).
Erw-garegog (Stony acre).
Erw-goch (Red acre).
Erw-hir (Long acre).
Erw-las (Green acre).
Erw-lom (Barren acre).
Erw-lon (Happy acre).
Erw'r clochydd (The sexton's acre).
Erw'r delyn (The harp's acre).
Erw'r efail (The acre of the forge).
Erw'r gwanwyn (The spring's acre).
Erw'r grug (Heather acre).
Erw'r pobydd (The baker's acre).
Erw-wastad (Flat acre).
Erw-wen (White acre).

Eryri (Snowdon).
This is an example of a place-name transferred as a house-name and probably a linguistic souvenir as well, brought back by the householders as a reminder of happy days spent mountaineering in this particular area of natural beauty in North Wales, with six peaks above 3,000 feet as well as Snowdon itself at 3,650 feet.

Esgair (Ridge or Spur of mountain).
The dwelling has a fine view of the mountain ridge ahead. The occupants record the feature in the house-name. It could also be a place-name in Carmarthenshire transferred as a house-name.

Related house-names:
Esgair ddu (Dark spur).
Esgair ganol (Middle ridge).
Esgair wen (White ridge).
Esgair-y-graig (The ridge of the rock).

Ewyn-gwyn (White foam).
The dwelling is on the coast facing the sea and the incoming breakers. Frothy white foam ebbs and flows around the rocky shoreline to the delight of the occupants. The house-name, at times, is washed by spray.
Related house-names:
Ewyn-y-don (The wave's foam).
Ewyn-y-môr (The sea's foam).

F

Faenol: Faenor. *See*: **Y Faenol: Y Faenor**.
Faenol-Fach. *See*: **Y Faenol-Fach**.
Faenol-Fawr. *See*: **Y Faenol-Fawr**.

Fagwr (Derived from **Magwr** – Stonewall, ruins, fortifications).
Ancient historical sites are important features and of much interest to many. The dwelling is situated near such a place and the house-name is a visible reminder of the struggles of earlier times.

Fannog, Y (The Hilltop).
Situation is seized upon by the house-holders. The house-name declares that the dwelling is close to or on the summit of the hill, safe and secure from the danger of flooding!

Fedwen arian, (Y) ((The) Silver birch tree).
The graceful birch with its silvery-white bark is a notable feature, its leaves golden in spring, green in summer and yellow in winter. The occupants appreciate its beauty and the house-name confirms the fact.
Related house-names:
Fedwen-aur, (Y) ((The) Golden birch tree).
Fedwen-fach, (Y) ((The) Little birch tree).

Felin-fach (Little mill).
The dwelling or part of it was initially a small mill. The house-name perpetuates the historical record. It is also a place-name near Lampeter, Ceredigion.
Related house-names:
Felinganol (Middle mill).
Also, a place-name in Pembrokeshire possibly connected with the occupants and transferred as a house-name.
Felin-newydd (New mill).
Felin-ucha(f) (Highest mill).
Felin-wen (White mill).
Also the name of a village near Carmarthen possibly transferred as a house-name.

Ffawydd (Beech trees).
The dwelling is situated close to a beech wood. In autumn especially, the occupants may observe these stately trees aglow with russet brown and flaming gold.
Related house-name:
Ffawyddog (Grove of beech trees; Beechen).
Also, possibly the name of a village near Crucywel (Crickhowell), Powys transferred as a house-name due to the occupants' personal connections.

Ffinnant (Boundary stream).
Boundaries have precise locations and rivers and streams are frequently dividing lines. This dwelling is near such a stream and the house-name records the fact.

Fforest-fach (Little forest).
The dwelling is adjacent to a small wood. The name is also that of a village and a locality on the outskirts of Swansea city and possibly transferred as a house-name.
Related house-name:
Fforest newydd (New forest).

Ffos-helyg (Willow ditch).
The house-name captures the feature: the willow trees beside the drainage ditch.
Related house-names:
Ffos-las (Green ditch).
Ffos-y-ffin (The boundary ditch).
Boundaries are important and this boundary is defined by the exact location of this ditch. This name is also that of a village near Henfynyw, Ceredigion and may well have been transferred as a cherished house-name.
Ffos-y-Gest (The Gest ditch).
Y Gest, the name of a hill near Tremadog, Gwynedd has been transferred as a house-name.
Ffosygïach (The snipe's ditch).
This place-name near Llannarth, Ceredigion has been transferred as a house-name.

Ffridd-fach (Small mountain pasture).
The house-name declares the location and defines its magnitude. This is a rural setting enjoyed by the householders.

Related house-names:
Ffridd-fawr (Large mountain pasture).
Ffridd-goch (Red mountain pasture).
Ffridd-wyllt (Wild mountain pasture).
Ffridd-wen (Pleasant mountain pasture).

Ffrwd-y-fâl (The mill-stream).
Location is reflected in the house-name. The dwelling is situated near the fast flowing mill-stream.
Related house-names:
Ffrwd-y-felin (The mill stream).
Ffrydiau (Rushing streams).
Ffrydiau-gwynion (White (rushing) streams).

Ffynhonnau (Springs; Fountains; Wells).
Wales abounds in springs, fountains and wells, many of which bear intriguing names: **Ffynnon chwerthin** (Laughter well); **Ffynnon lefrith** (Milk well); **Ffynnon y cythraul** (The devil's well); **Ffynnon y fil feibion** (Well of the Holy Innocents); **Pistyll y blaidd** (The wolf's spring) . . . The house-name suggests that there are several wells in close proximity to the dwelling.
Related house-names:
Ffynnon cadno (Fox's well).
Ffynnonddewi (One of more than thirty wells dedicated to Dewi, Patron Saint of Wales).
The dwelling probably abuts the site of one of these wells. It could possibly be a house-name derived from the transference of the name of a village near Llandysiliogogo, Ceredigion.
Ffynnon-ddrain (Thorn well).
This could also be the transference of the name of the

village near the town of Carmarthen and now used as a house-name.
Ffynnon-ddwrgi (Otter's well).
Ffynnongroyw (Fresh spring or well).
This could also be an example of place-name (a village near Llanasa, Flintshire) transferred as a house-name.
Ffynnon Iago (Iago's well).
The dwelling is situated near one of the three wells bearing this name: Cilmaenllwyd, Pembrokeshire; Llanllawddog parish or Llanybydder parish, both in Carmarthenshire.
Ffynnon-oer (Cold well).
Ffynnon-saer (Carpenter's well).
Ffynnon-wen (Blessed well).
The dwelling takes its name from one of two noted healing wells: Llan-lwy parish, Pembrokeshire or Henllan parish, Denbighshire.
Ffynnon-y-gwyddau (The geese's well).

Foel, Y (The bare hill (top)).
Not all hills are wooded. This dwelling is situated on or near this bleak hilltop, which the occupants use as a feature to identify their property.
   Related house-names:
Foel-allt, Y (The bare (treeless) hillside).
Foelas (Bare green hilltop).

Foty, Y (The summer dwelling in the uplands).
See: **Hafoty**.

Fron, Y ((The) hillside).
The hills of Wales are many, so are the dwellings on the hillsides. The house-name locates the position of the house.

Perhaps the name may have been transferred from the village near Brymbo, Wrecsam C.B., due to family connections.
Related house-names:
Frondeg (Fair hillside).
Fron-dderw (Oak hillside).
Fron-fedw (Birch-tree hillside).
Fron-friallu (Primrose hillside).
Fron-goch (Red hillside).
Fron-heulog (Sunny hillside).
Fron-las (Green hillside).
Fron-lwyd (Grey hillside).
Fron-olau (Light hillside).
Fron-wen (White hillside).

G

Gadlas (A glade, a green).
The dwelling stands on a site which was originally a clear open space. The house-name reminds the casual observer of this notable fact.

Gaeafdy (Winter dwelling).
The owners occupy this property as a winter retreat. Some people have summer houses, some have . . .
Related house-names:
Gaeafle (Winter quarters).
Gaeafwynt (Winter wind).

Galwad-y-môr (Call of the sea).
The dwelling is close to the sea-shore and the occupants yearn as did John Masefield:

*'I must go down to the seas again, for the call of the
   running tide
Is a wild call and a clear call that may not be denied . . .'*
                                                   Sea Fever

Gardd Nain (Grandmother's garden).
Many houses have gardens. This house has a special garden. A cherished member of the family planted it and its beauty and fragrance still remain.
   Unrelated house-name:
Gardden (from **cardden** = enclosure, fort; thicket).

Garn, Y (The cairn or barrow).
The house-name may record the local site of an historic cairn. Also, a mountain near Llanberis, Gwynedd, and a parish and village in Pembrokeshire bear the same name. The occupants may have transferred one of these locations as a linguistic souvenir of previous happy occasions.
   Related house-names:
Garn Bach (Small cairn or barrow).
Also, the name of a mountain in Gwynedd.
Garn Goch (Red cairn or barrow).
Also, the name of a district near Fforest-fach, Swansea.
Garn-wen (White cairn or barrow).

Garreg wen (White stone; quartz stone).
The house-name is derived from a prominent feature in the locality. The white stone is clearly visible and the house-holders identify their address with it.

Garth (Field; enclosure).
The house-name has an historical aspect. The dwelling

stands now on ground that was some form of enclosure in the past. Also, it is the name of a village near Treflys, Powys and could possibly have been transferred as a house-name due to some family connections with this village.

Gelert (Prince Llywelyn's dog).
Attention is drawn by this unusual house-name to the oft told story of the utter faithfulness of this dog to its master, and is further perpetuated by the village and parish of **Beddgelert** (Gelert's grave), Gwynedd.

Gelli-aur (Golden grove).
An idyllic spot to dwell. The flowers and foliage are golden in the sunshine and the householders are delighted with their house-name (also a place-name near Carmarthen).
Related house-names:
Gelli-dawel (Quiet or peaceful grove).
Gelli-deg (Fair or beautiful grove).
Gelli-dywyll (Dark grove).
Gellifach (Small grove).
Gelli-fedw (Grove of birch trees).
Gelli-gron (Round grove).
Gelli-haf (Summer grove).
Gelli-lon (Happy grove).
Gelli-lwyd (Grey grove).
Gelli-wastad (Grove on flat ground).
Gelli-wen (White grove).
Gelli-werdd (Green grove).

Gerallt (Near a wooded hillside).
With this house-name the occupants further clarify the

location by identifying the dwelling with a known feature in the locality. This is also a male Christian name.
Related house-names:
Gerllwyn (Near a bush).
Gernant (Near a stream).
Ger-y-castell (Near the castle).
Ger-y-coed (Near the wood).
Ger-y-felin (Near the mill).
Ger-y-llan (Near the church).
Ger-y-lli (Near the sea).
Ger-y-maes (Near the field).
Ger-y-môr (Near the sea).
Ger-yr-ywen (Near the yew-tree).
Ger-y-twˆr (Near the tower).

Gerddi, Y (The Gardens).
The occupants of this property cultivate more than *one* garden. Evidently they have green fingers and their flowers, fruit and vegetables are luxuriant.
Related house-name:
Gerddi-gleision (Green gardens).

Gilfach-glyd. *See*: **Y Gilfach-glyd**.

Glan-dwˆr (River bank).
The house-name indicates that the dwelling is situated on the river bank. A relevant post code and an ordnance survey map would indicate which river. It could perhaps be a transferred place-name of a district on the outskirts of Swansea or that of a village and an area in Pembrokeshire.
Related house-names:
Glanffrwd (Bank of stream).

Glan-nant (Brook side).

Glan-rhyd (Edge or side of ford).

Also the name of a village near Cardigan, Ceredigion; one near Llanwnda and another due south of Morfa Nefyn – both in Gwynedd, possibly transferred as a house-name.

Glan-y-coed (Tree lined hillside).

Glan-y-gors (Edge of the marsh).

Glan-y-môr (The sea-shore).

Glan-y-nant (Bank of the stream).

Glanyrafon (The river bank: The river side).

There is also the possibility of a transference of this place-name which is shared by two villages in Flintshire.

Glasbant (Green hollow).

The house-name indicates the location of the dwelling: in a verdant hollow.

Related house-names:

Glasdir (Green land (fields)).

Glasfor (Blue sea).

Glasfryn (Green hill).

Also the name of a village in Conwy County Borough and possibly transferred as a house-name.

Glasgoed (Green trees).

Also the name of a district in Monmouthshire and that of a village near Llanrug, Gwynedd possibly transferred as a house-name.

Glaslwyn (Green bush).

Glasnant (Green valley or stream).

Glas-y-dorlan (Kingfisher).

Glesni (Blueness; greenness).

Azure skies and verdant pastures are brought to mind by

this house-name, with summer breezes wafting around the dwelling in an idyllic rural setting or perhaps beside the sea – the very stuff of paradise. (Also a female's name.)

Glyn (Glen, narrow valley).
The property stands in the narrow valley or in full view of it. The occupants perhaps have close ties with a parish of this name in Powys and may have transferred the place-name as a house-name.

Related house-names:
Glynawelon (Glen or valley of breezes).
Glyn-celyn (Holly glen).
Glyn-collen (Hazel glen).
Glen-deri (Oak glen).
Glyn-derwen (Oak-tree glen).
Glyn-eithin (Gorse glen).
Glyn-hir (Long glen).
This is also a name of a district in Pontarddulais, Swansea, that may be transferred as a house-name.
Glyn-tawel (Quiet glen).
Glyn-teg (Beautiful glen).
Glyn-Rhosyn (Rose glen).
Glyn-y-coed (Wooded glen).
Glyn-yr-hebog (The falcon's glen).
Glyn-yr-ŵyn (The lambs' glen).

Godre'r-graig (Foot of the rock).
The situation of the dwelling near the bottom of a massive rock may have prompted the occupants. Again, the name of a village near Ystalyfera, in the Swansea valley may have been transferred as a house-name due to family ties with that area.

Related house-names:
Godre'r coed (The lower edge of the wood).
Godre'r grug (The lower edge of the heather-line).

Goedwig, Y (The forest).
A simple and straightforward house-name depicting the precise location of the dwelling: near or within the forest. *See*: **Gwigfa**.

Golwg-y-bryn (View of the hill).
From the dwelling the view is splendid. The occupants see the distant hill and this adds a vital perspective to their daily outlook.
Related house-names:
Golwg-y-cwm (View of the valley).
Golwg-y-môr (View of the sea).
Golwg-yr-afon (View of the river).
Golwg-y-wawr (View of the dawn).
Golygfa-deg (Beautiful view).

Gorllewinwynt (Westerly wind).
With this house-name the occupants acknowledge a wind that frequently registers Force 6 or more on the Beaufort scale.

Gorswen (White marsh).
The view from the dwelling encompasses marshland covered with cuckoo flowers or common cottongrass and prompts the occupants to adopt this apt house-name.

Gorwel (Horizon).
A city sky-line, a tranquil seascape, a mountain range of

challenging peaks . . . to each his own. The occupants are pleased with the view and confirm this with their house-name.
Related house-name:
Gorwel-deg (Fair horizon).

Graeanfa (Gravelly soil).
The occupants have chosen a house-name that classifies the soil around the dwelling. There may yet be a future for growbags.

Graig-goch (Red rock).
The view from the dwelling is magnificent. The rock, red in the sunset is splendid. The house-name is fitting. It could also be the transferred name of a cliff near Tal-y-llyn, Gwynedd due to family ties with that area.
Related house-names:
Graig las (Green rock).
Also the name of a cliff near Brithdir, Gwynedd.
Graig wen (White rock).
Also the name of a mountain near Maentwrog, Gwynedd.

Gronant (Pebbles of a stream).
Smooth pebbles from a nearby stream have been used to decorate a pathway or wall at the residence and provide the householders with a distinctive house-name.

Grugfryn (Heather hill).
The view from the dwelling is dominant and the house-holders confirm this in the house-name.
Related house-name:
Grug-y-mynydd (Mountain heather).

Gurnos (Cone-shaped hill).
The house-name may describe the view from the dwelling. It may also declare a family connection between the occupants and a village of that name located between Ystalyfera and Ystradgynlais in the Swansea valley.

Gwahoddiad (Invitation).
Some questions are implied: Did the occupants receive an invitation to reside here initially, or do they now offer an invitation to all and sundry to call and visit them?

Gwalia (Wales – a name first used in the Middle Ages).
With this house-name the householders proudly declare that their dwelling and its environs are wholly part of Wales (Cymru).

Gwâl-ysgyfarnog (A hare's form (lair)).
The dwelling is obviously situated near the form of a hare, which is a kind of bed hidden in a bush or briar patch. The householders delight in observing this animal which is one of the gentlest of all mammals.

Gwarallt (Ground just above and behind a hill or wood).
The view from the dwelling may be reflected in the house-name or the dwelling itself is situated on upper ground beyond a wood.
   Related house-names:
Gwar-bryn (Upper part of hill).
Gwarclawdd (Slope above (boundary) dyke).
Gwar-coed (Slope above a wood).
Gwar-cwm (Upper part of a valley).
Gwarffynnon (Slope above a fountain).

Gwarmynydd (Upper part of mountain).
Gwar-nant (Upper bank of brook).
Gwar-y-castell (The castle hill-side).
Gwar-y-ddôl (The meadow bank).
Gwar-y-felin (Hill-side behind the mill).

Gwaungwaddod (Moles' moorland).
This house-name describes well the precise nature of the terrain near the dwelling. The land is dotted about with many molehills, evidence of their unsolicited industry.

Gwe-corryn (Spider's web, cobweb).
Not the usual traditional house-name for these householders. Here is one that is different and distinctive.

Gweddi (Prayer).
Pride of place is given to prayer in this house and it is openly admitted by the occupants, whose lives are wholly committed to God – 'that than which no greater can be conceived'.

Gwêl-fôr (Sight of (the) sea).
The sea may be viewed from the dwelling. Hence the house-name.
   Related house-names:
Gwêl-fro (Sight of (the) vale).
Gwêl-fryn (Sight of (the) hill).
Gwêl Rheidol (Sight of (the River) Rheidol).
Gwêl-y-don (Sight of the wave).

Gwenffrwd (Stream of turbulent white-water).
The house-name refers to a rushing stream of white-water

close to the dwelling. This feature provides the householders with an apt name.

Gwenfro (Fair or blessed land or region, paradise).
The householders declare that this is *the place* to live. They rejoice in the house-name.

Gwenith-gwyn (White wheat).
White wheat-fields in late summer and early autumn are clearly seen from the dwelling and account for the house-name.

Gwên-yr-haul (The sun's smile).
The householders are fortunate that the dwelling has a sunny aspect. This is confirmed by the house-name.
Related house-name:
Gwên-y-wawr (The dawn's smile).

Gwersyll (A camp).
Homes like occupants appear in all shapes and sizes. Some people consider their homes as castles, others as hideaways. These dwellers have no illusions, theirs is just a camp!

Gwesbyr (Westbury).
A place-name, initially Westbury but corrupted by the passage of time now appears as Gwesbyr, a village near Prestatyn, Flintshire and transferred here as a house-name.

Gwesty'r adar (Birds' hotel).
The occupants of this dwelling relish the song of the blackbird, the twittering of sparrows, the cooing of doves, the comings and goings of magpies . . . They also love birds

and probably encourage them with seeds, crumbs and a fresh supply of water.

Gweunydd (Moorlands).
This house-name emphasises the location of the dwelling which is situated on and surrounded by moorland.

Gwigfa (Forest).
The house-name reveals that the location of the dwelling is in a clearing surrounded by trees of the forest. The householders are wholly satisfied with their straightforward labelling

Gwrthwynt (Cross-wind).
The exposed site on which the dwelling stands is buffeted savagely by northerlies and westerlies. The occupants accept what cannot be changed and soldier on resolutely.

Gwylfa (An observation post; a watching-place).
The householders may be astronomers or ornithologists or empirical sociologists or . . . Perhaps they just want to watch the rest of the world go by from the security of their home.

Gwynfa (Blessed land, paradise).
The householders have arrived at the zenith of their aspirations. This is the very location and the dwelling of their dreams. The house-name conveys their exuberance!
Related house-names:
Gwynfryn (Blessed height, holy mount; white mount).
Also the name of a village near Mwynglawdd, Wrecsam County Borough, (and a male Christian name).
Gwynlais (White stream).

Gwyrddgoed (Green trees).
Location is defined by this house-name. The dwelling is situated near or in the green wood.
Related house-names:
Gwyrddle (Green open space).
Gwyrddfan (Green place).

H

Hafal (Equal).
Does this house-name imply that the householders believe whole heartedly in the equality of the sexes and of equal opportunities for all? If so, it may herald the beginning of a new dawn and the demise of sexism, racism, ageism . . .

Hafan (Haven, harbour).
The dwellers consider that their home provides them with a safe haven during the perilous storms of life – an important attribute of the ideal home.
Related house-names:
Hafan-deg (Fair haven).
Hafan-yr-heliwr (The hunter's haven).
Hafan-y-wennol (The swallow's haven).

Hafod (Summer residence in the uplands).
An upland farmstead formerly occupied by the family and its livestock during the summer months only, and where grazing was practised to a greater extent than cultivation. This house-name recalls an earlier history – 15th to the 19th century. It could also be an example of a place-name transferred as a house-name, either that of a village in the

County Borough of Rhondda Cynon Taf or a district in the city of Swansea. *See*: **Hendre**.

Related house-names:

Hafod-aur (Golden summer residence).

Hafod-hudol (Magical summer residence).

Hafod-lon (Happy summer residence).

Hafod-lwyd (Grey summer residence).

Hafod-newydd (New summer residence).

Hafod-oer (Cold summer residence).

Hafod-unnos (Historically – a dwelling built overnight on common land (conferring right of abode on the builder)). *See*: **Tŷ unnos**.

Hafod-y-cadno (The fox's summer residence).

Hafod-y-coed (The forest's summer residence).

Hafod-y-gân (The song's summer residence).

Hafod-y-gog (The cuckoo's summer residence).

Hafod-y-grug (The heather's summer residence).

Hafod-y-wennol (The swallow's summer residence).

Hafod-yr-ŵyn (The lambs' summer residence).

Hafoty (Summer house in the uplands).

Optimists thankfully still abound and the occupants are to be numbered with them. Their choice of house-name will bring a smile to many faces on chilly wintry days.

Hamdden (Leisure).

The occupants of this dwelling believe in the old maxim: 'All work and no play makes Jack a dull boy.' Leisure must be a vital element in the ideal home. They also agree with the thoughts expressed in W. H. Davies's poem on the same topic:

> *'What is this life if, full of care,*
> *we have no time to stand and stare?'*

Hanner-ffordd (Half-way).
An intriguing house-name. Is the dwelling half-way between two notable points? Are the inhabitants in their happiness half-way between heaven and earth? One wonders.

Haul-y-bore (The morning sun).
Directly descriptive, this house-name refers to the sunny position of the dwelling. It receives direct sunlight especially from dawn till noon.
Related house-names:
Haul-y-bryn (The hill's sun).
Haul-y-môr (The sea's sun).

Hawddamor (Good luck! Blessing!).
With this friendly greeting the householders reveal their good will to all who pass by. Long may it prevail.

Hebog-y-dyffryn (The valley's hawk).
The householders are keen ornithologists and follow carefully the flight of the hawk along the valley. The dwelling affords them an excellent observation post and their vigils are well rewarded by this local bird of prey.

Heddfan (Place of peace).
Every home should be one. The occupants advertise the fact that tranquillity is a cherished feature in their home.
Related house-names:
Hedd-fryn (Hill of peace).

Heddle (Place of peace).
Heddlys (Police court, Magistrates' court).
Heddwch (Peace, tranquillity).

Hen-aelwyd (Old hearth or home).
Tradition and continuity are implied by this house-name, generations of the same family may have been born and brought up on this very spot. A sense of history has been forged here.
Related house-names:
Hen-ardd (Old garden).
Hen-blas (Old mansion).
Hen-dafarn (Old tavern).
Hen dderwen (Old oak-tree).
Hendre (Old family home; winter farmstead in the lowlands).
Winter dwelling located in the valley to which the family and its sheep and cattle returned after the summer period at Hafod in the uplands.
The location, the building or the historical tradition connected to this house-name may have influenced the occupants in their choice. *See*: **Hafod**.
Hendre-fawr (Large old family home).
Hendre-uchaf (Highest old family home).
Hendy. *See*: **Yr Hendy**.
Hen-dŷ-gwair (Old hayshed).
Hen-efail (Old smithy or forge).
Henfro (Land of one's infancy).
Henfryn (Old hill).
Henffald (Old animal pound).
Hengwrt (Old court or mansion).

Hen-gynefin (Old haunt, old familiar dwelling).

Henllan (Old enclosure).

Also possibly, the transfer of either the name of a parish and village in Denbighshire or the name of a village in Ceredigion.

Henllys (Old court, hall or mansion).

Also possibly, the transfer of the name of a parish in Monmouthshire.

Hen-ysgol ((Old school).

Heulwen-haf (Summer sunshine).

There is no substitute for the halcyon days of warm summer. The house-name reminds the occupants throughout the year of that joyous season.

Hiraeth (Longing, yearning).

The householders, by using the house-name, raise an important issue. For what do we yearn: riches, position, peace, health, beauty, yester-year . . .?

Hir-aros (A long stay).

This house-name declares the fervent hope of the dwelling's occupants, that each will live well beyond the stipulated age of threescore years and ten.

Related house-names:

Hirfryn (Long hill).

Hirllwyn (Long grove or wood).

Hirnant (Long stream).

Huanfa (Sunny place).

Situation dictates the house-name in this instance. The dwelling stands on a sunny spot and the occupants rejoice.

Hudol-fan (Magical place).
The householders have succeeded in finding a magical place to live. Such is their joy that they wish to inform everyone via the house-name.

Hud-y-machlud (Magic of the sunset).
'When day is done and shadows fall . . .' and the bustling booming world begins to quieten, the dwelling takes on a mysterious aura and the setting sun adds a touch of glory to eventide. The householders are thrilled.

Hyfryd-ddewis (A beautiful choice).
This intriguing house-name begs the question: Whose? Was it her choice, or his, or their choice? What really matters is that the occupants are happy with their home.
   Related house-name:
Hyfrydle (Beautiful place).

I

Iet-fawr (Large gate).
Gates of properties are frequently distinctive features. In this instance it is not colour but size that is emphasised by the house-name.
   Related house-names:
Iet-goch (Red gate).
Iet-wen (White gate).
Iet-yr-hendy (Gate of the old house).

Isallt (Below a hill; Below a wood).
Location influences the choice of house-name. This dwelling stands below a hill or woods.

Related house-names:

Is-coed (Below a wood).
This could also be an example of a place-name (a parish in Flintshire), transferred as a house-name.
Isfryn (Below a hill).
Islwyn (Below a bush).
This is also a popular male Christian name.
Is-y-ffynnon (Below the fountain).
Is-y-gaer (Below the fort).
Is-y-garn (Below the cairn).
Isygarreg (Below the stone or rock).
Is-yr-allt (Below the hill; Below the wood).
Is-y-wenallt (Below the white hill).

Iorwg (Ivy).
The ivy covered walls of the house give it a homely charm that pleases the occupants.

L

Llaethdy (A dairy).
The house-name probably refers to an earlier use of the building. It is also the name of a region at Llanbadarn Fynydd, Powys and may be an example of a place-name transferred as a house-name.

Llafur (Labour).
Wales has long been a home to radicalism. Most of its people readily express political opinions. Are the house-holders, with this house-name, declaring their Party affiliation or revealing the formula necessary in order that a dwelling may retain its beauty and attractiveness?

Llain (A narrow piece or parcel of land).
The dwelling is situated on a narrow strip of ground.
   Related house-names:
Llain-deg (A beautiful strip of land).
Llain-felen (Yellow strip of land).
Llain-goch (Red strip of land).
This is also the name of a village near Holyhead, Anglesey and could well be an example of a place-name transferred as a house-name for personal reasons.
Llain-wen (White or fair strip of land).
Llain-y-brenin (The king's strip of land).
Llain-y-delyn (The harp's strip of land).

Llais-y-gwynt (Voice or sound of the wind).
With this house-name the householders note the plaintive cry of the wind as it wreathes its way around the dwelling.
   Related house-names:
Llais-y-môr (Voice or sound of the sea).
Llais-y-nant (Voice or sound of the stream).
Llais-yr-afon (Voice or sound of the river).
Llais-yr-awel (Voice or sound of the breeze).

Llandre (Site of former dwelling place).
The house-name may declare that the present dwelling stands on a time-honoured site. Then again, it may be a transference of the name of a village in Ceredigion or one of two in Carmarthenshire, due to the personal interests of the householders.
   Related house-names:
Llandinam (The church near the small fort).
An example of a place-name (that of a parish and village in

Powys originally **Llandinan**), transferred as a house-name due to the householders personal ties with that area.
Llanfair (Church of St. Mary).
Also the name of a parish and village in Gwynedd and that of a locality in Monmouthshire.
Llanfechan (Small church or enclosure).
Also the name of a locality at Tregynon, Powys.

Llawenydd (Joy, happiness).
Happiness like measles is infectious. Happy people make a happy place and share their joy with others. The house-name indicates the occupants' state of mind.
Related house-name:
Llawen-fan (Happy place).

Llecyn (Small plot of land).
The dwelling is situated on a small piece or parcel of land. In the opinion of the occupants 'small is beautiful'.
Related house-names:
Llecyn-y-llan (The church's small enclosure).
Llecyn-yr-haul (The sun's small plot of land).

Llety-cariad (Love's abode).
One of the attributes of an ideal home is that love, an abiding unconditional love, is constantly present. With this house-name the occupants proudly declare it is so.
Related house-names:
Llety-celyn (Holly-covered dwelling).
Llety-clyd (Cosy dwelling).
Llety-derw (Oak dwelling).
Llety-dryw (Wren's nest).
Llety-gwyn (White dwelling).

Llety-hebog (Hawk's nest).
Llety-heulog (Sunny dwelling).
Llety Iolo (Iolo's abode).
Llety-lleian (Nun's dwelling).
Llety-llygoden (Mouse's nest).
Llety Mair (Mair's abode).
Llety-mawr (Huge dwelling).
Llety-mieri (Dwelling place of brambles and briars).
Llety-morfil (Whale's dwelling).
This house-name found inland many miles from the sea, is probably a corrupted version of its original form: '*Llety Morfydd*' (Morfydd's dwelling).
Llety-teg (Beautiful dwelling).
Llety-tirion (Gentle dwelling).
Llety'n y llwyn (Dwelling in the grove).
Llety'r bugail (The shepherd's dwelling).
Llety'r Cymro (The Welshman's abode).
Llety'r eos (The nightingale's nest).
Llety'r gog (The cuckoo's nest).

Llun-y-mynydd (The mountain's picture).
The striking view from the dwelling, in this instance is that of Carn Ingli. The house-name suggests that the occupants enjoy the scenic beauty.

Llwyn (Bush; Grove; Woods).
An attractive bush or grove near the dwelling is seen as the significant feature by the householders and gives rise to the house-name. **Llwyn** is also the name of a village beyond Offa's dyke (*Clawdd Offa*), south of Bishop's Castle, Shropshire. It may well be an example of a place-name transferred as a house-name due to family connections.

Related house-names:
Llwyn-arian (Silver bush).
Llwyn-banadl (Broom bush).
Llwyn-bedw (Birch grove).
There is also the village of **Llwynbedw**, Cwmgiedd, Ystradgynlais, Powys that may have been transferred as a house-name.
Llwyncoed (Grove; Cluster of trees).
Llwyn-crychydd (Heron's woods).
Llwyndafydd (Dafydd's woods).
Also the name of a village, near New Quay, Ceredigion.
Llwyn-del (Pretty bush).
Llwyn-derw (Oak-grove).
Also the name of a village near Welshpool (Y Trallwng), Powys.
Llwyn-drain (Thorn bush).
Llwyn-dyrys (Bramble thicket).
Also the name of a village, east of Nefyn, Llŷn Peninsula.
Llwyn-eiddew (Ivy bush).
Llwyn-eithin (Gorse bush).
Llwyn-eryr (Eagle's bush).
Llwyn-ffynnon (Well's bush).
Llwyn-glas (Green bush).
Llwyn-gron (Round grove).
Llwyn-helyg (Willow grove).
Llwyn-hudol (Enchanting bush).
Llwyn-hyfryd (Beautiful bush).
Llwyni (Bushes).
Llwyn-iorwg (Ivy bush).
Llwyn llinos (Linnet's bush).
Llwynmawr (Huge bush).
Also the name of a village near Wrexham.
Llwynmeudwy (Hermit's grove).

Llwyn-onn (Ash grove).
In addition it is the name of a village near New Quay, Ceredigion and that of a popular air for the harp.
Llwyn-rhedyn (Clump of bracken).
Llwyn-teg (Beautiful bush).
Llwynwern (Alder grove).
Llwyn-y-berllan (The orchard grove).
Llwyn-y-brain (The crows' grove).
Llwyn-y-gog (The cuckoo's grove).
Llwyn-y-piod (The magpies' grove).
Llwyn-yr-eos (The nightingale's grove).
Llwyn-yr-haf (The summer's grove).

Llys-alaw (Melody's court).
The house-name declares that music is of paramount importance in the lives of the occupants.
  Related house-names:
Llys-cerdd (Music's court; Poetry's court).
Llys-eryr (Eagle's court).
Llys-gwyn (White court).
Llys-hedd (Peace court).
Llys-helyg (Willow court).
Llys Neifion (Neptune's court)
Llysnewydd (New court).
Llys-wen (White court).
This is also the name of a parish and village to the north of Brecon, Powys.
Llys-y-coed (The forest court).
Llys-y-dryw (The wren's court).
Llys-y-frân (The crow's court).
Also the name of a parish and village due north of Clarbeston Road, Pembrokeshire.

Llys-y-graig (The rock's court).
Llys-y-gwynt (The wind's court).
Llys-yr-awel (The breeze's court).
Llys-yr-haul (The sun's court).
Llys-yr-hebog (The hawk's court).
Llys-yr-wylan (The gull's court).
Llys-y-wennol (The swallow's court).

M

Maengwyn (White stone).
A large white stone is a significant feature in the neighbourhood and the householders seize the opportunity to identify their property with it.
Related house-names:
Maen-llwyd (Grey stone).
Maen-melin (Millstone).
Maenol: Maenor. *See*: **Y Faenol**.
Maen-y-groes (Stone of the cross).
See: **Meini**.

Maerdy (Historically – a summer dwelling for tending cattle).
With this house-name the householders reveal part of the history related to their dwelling.

Maesawelon (Field of the breezes).
Breezes galore constantly caress the greenfield site where the dwelling stands. The house-name confirms the situation.
Related house-names:
Maeseglwys (Church field).

Maes-glas (Green field).
Maes-gwyn (White field).
Maes-hyfryd (Beautiful field).
Maes-mawr (Huge field).
Maesmelyn (Yellow field).
Maesteg (Pretty field; Fair field).
This could also be an example of a place-name transferred as a house-name. **Maesteg** is a town in the County Borough of Bridgend.
Maes-tŷ-mawr (Mansion field).
Maes-y-bedol (The horseshoe field).
Maes-y-bont (The bridge field).
Also the name of a village near Llanarthne, Carmarthenshire.
Maes-y-coed (The forest field).
Maes-y-cregyn (The seashells' field).
Maes-y-dderwen (The oak-tree field).
Maes-y-deri (The oak-wood field).
Maes-y-felin (The mill-field).
Maes-y-ffynnon (The spring field).
Maes-y-gelynnen (The holly-tree field).
Maes-y-goron (The crown's field).
Maesymeillion (The clover field).
This could also be an example of a place-name transferred as a house-name. **Maesymeillion** is the name of a locality near Llandysul, Ceredigion.
Maes-yr-efail (The forge field).
Maes-yr-haul (The sun's field).
Maes-y-rhiw (The hill field).
Maes-yr-onnen (The ash-tree field).
Maes-y-prior (The Priory field).

Maes-y-wawr (The dawn's field).
Maes-y-wern (The alder-wood field).

Man-aros (Permanent place).
An important aspect of home is its stability. The householders declare this hearth to be so.
   Related house-names:
Mandel (Pretty place).
Mandinam (Faultless or perfect place).
Man-gwyn (Blessed place; White place).
Man-hyfryd (Beautiful place).
Manoer (Cold place).

Meifod (Middle residence).
This could be the house-name of a middle dwelling. It could also be an example of a place-name transferred as a house-name. **Meifod** is a parish and a village near Welshpool, Powys.

Meillion (Clover).
Apart from grass, the verdant pasture around the dwelling contains an abundance of buttercup, dandelion, coltsfoot, clover . . .

Meini (Stones).
The house-name refers to the main materials used in the construction of the dwelling.
   Related house-names:
Meini-diddos (Sheltering stones).
Meini-gwynion (White stones).
Meini-llwydion (Grey stones).

Melin-y-coed (The forest mill).
The house-name locates and indicates the former use of the building. Also, possibly it could be an example of the transference of a place-name. **Melin-y-coed** is a village, near the County Borough of Conwy.
   Related house-names:
Melin-y-ddôl (The meadow mill).
Melin-y-wig (The forest mill).
Also possibly an example of the transference of a place-name as a house-name. **Melin-y-wig** is a village, near Gwyddelwern, Denbighshire.

Melodi (Melody).
Life in this house is seen as one harmonious continuum.

Melys-dref (Sweet home).
With this house-name the householders express delight with their abode. *See*: **Cartref**.

Mesen-fach (Small acorn).
'Tall oaks from little acorns . . .' The future expectations implied are truly great.

Meysydd (Fields; Open country).
Originally the dwelling stood serenely amongst green fields. By today urbanisation has overtaken the rural scene.

Min-afon (River bank).
The house-name may refer to the precise location of the dwelling or to the view enjoyed by the occupants.
   Related house-names:
Mindraeth (Edge of shore).
Minffordd (Wayside).

Minfor (Seashore; Seaside).
Min-y-cae (Edge of the field).
Min-y-coed (Edge of the wood).
Min-y-ddôl (Edge of the pasture).
Min-y-don (Edge of the wave).
Min-y-ffrwd (Edge of the torrent).
Min-y-glyn (Side of the glen).
Min-y-grug (Edge of the heather).
Min-y-gwynt (Keen edge of the wind).
Min-y-môr (Seashore; Seaside).
Minymynydd (Brow of the mountain).
Min-yr-awel (Keenness of the breeze).

Môr-allt (Sea cliff).
The location is maritime and the view spectacular with the cliff rising from the waves. This prominent feature inspires the householders to incorporate it in the house-name.
Relevant house-names:
Môr-awel (Sea breeze).
Môr-awelon (Sea breezes).
Môr-ewyn (Sea foam).
Morfa (Salt marsh; Marsh; Moor).
Môr-o-gariad ('A sea of love'/Much love).
Môr-olwg (Sea view).

Muriau (Walls).
Walls can be divisive structures. Here in this dwelling they enclose the occupants in a safe and secure environment.

Murmur-y-coed ((The) murmur of the trees).
The location of the dwelling enables the occupants to hear the sound of the rustling leaves on the neighbouring trees.

Related house-names:
Murmur y dail ((The) murmur of the leaves).
Murmur-y-gwynt ((The) murmur of the wind).
Murmur-y-llanw ((The) murmur of the tide).
Murmur-y-meysydd ((The) murmur of the fields).
Murmur-y-môr ((The) murmur of the sea).
Murmur-y-nant ((The) murmur of the stream).

Mwswm-gwyn (White moss).
The view from the property is of a grove of oak-trees covered with a form of whitish moss (goat's moss?) – a distinctive house-name.

Mwynfan (Gentle place).
The low hills and gently undulating plains viewed from the dwelling suggest this apt house-name.

Mwythus (Sumptuous; Luxurious).
This is not merely a dwelling but a magnificently comfortable home, according to the occupants.

Mynachlog (Monastery).
This house-name may well refer to an earlier use of the site on which the present dwelling stands.

Mynydd-bach (Small mountain).
Location is paramount as is indicated by the house-name and refers either to the position of the dwelling or the view from it. Also, it is possibly an example of the transference of a place-name as a house-name. **Mynydd-bach** is the name

of a village on the outskirts of Swansea City and that of a Monmouthshire village, near Chepstow.

Mysg y meysydd (Among the fields; In the open country).
Surrounded by green pastures, the house-name describes the idyllic location of the dwelling.

N

Nanhyfer (Nevern).
This is an example of an earlier place-name in Pembrokeshire (**Nanhyfer**) transferred as a house-name by householders with strong ties with today's village of Nevern.

Nanteos (Nightingale valley).
The property situated in this particular valley is atuned regularly to the song of the nightingale.
Related house-names:
Nant Felys (Sweet stream or valley).
Also the name of a brook at Abergwili, Carmarthen.
Nantgaredig (Beloved valley).
Also the name of a village near Abergwili, Carmarthen.
Nantoer (Cold stream).
Nant-y-barcud (Valley of the kite).
Nant-y-brithyll (Stream of the trout).
Nant-y-ci (Valley of the dog).
Nant-y-deri (Valley of the oaks).
Nant-y-frân (Stream or valley of the crow).
Nant-y-ffin (Stream of the border).
Nant-y-gloch (Stream or valley of the bell).
Nant-y-llyn (Stream of the lake).

Nant-y-milwr (Valley of the soldier).
Nant-y-mynydd (The mountain stream).
Nantyrarian (Stream or valley of the silver).
Nant-y-wenynen (Stream or valley of the bee).

Nefoedd-fach (Little heaven).
The occupants have no hesitation in declaring that home is tranquillity itself and a joy of joys.

Neuadd (Hall or mansion).
The building itself is impressive and merits its precise house-name. It is also the name of two villages, one near Llanarth, Ceredigion, the other near Llangamarch Wells, Powys possibly transferred as a house-name.
   Related house-names:
Neuadd-deg (Beautiful hall or mansion).
Neuadd-hen (Old hall or mansion).
Neuadd-fawr (Large hall or mansion).
Neuadd-lwyd (Grey hall or mansion).
Neuadd-newydd (New hall or mansion).
Neuadd-wen (White hall or mansion).

Newidfa (Exchange).
This house-name suggests that the ideal house is a venue for exchange: tranquillity for busyness; freshness for weariness; hope for despair; warmth for chilliness . . .

Nid-aros (Not remaining).
The householders declare emphatically that this is not to be their permanent address. They may have itching heels, suffer from wanderlust . . .

Niwl-y-bryn (The hill fog).
A descriptive house-name usually extols some positive attribute of the property. The above house-name does the opposite. Hilly terrain has many advantages but hill fog can be extremely detrimental.
Related house-names:
Niwl-y-môr (The sea fog).
Niwl-y-mynydd (The mountain fog).
Niwl-yr-hwyr (The evening mist).

Nodded (Shelter, sanctuary, protection).
A home provides more by far than a mere 'bolthole' for its occupants. This house-name infers that within its walls there exists a sanctuary from the strains of daily living.

Noddfa (Refuge).
The house-name confirms that the occupants give a high priority to the provision of shelter, safety and security in their home. (Several Welsh Nonconformist Chapels bear the name *Noddfa*.)

Noswyl (Period of rest after completing the day's work).
This house-name is a constant reminder to the householders of the comforts that await them once the mundane daily tasks have been completed and day is done, shadows fall and evening comes.

Nyddfa (Spinner's workshop).
The building once served as part of a flourishing rural economy. The house-name is an apt reminder of earlier times.

Nyth, Y (The nest).
The concept of home as a nest is a familiar one where parents together set up the place, the young are raised there, comings and goings are the order of the day, and usually it is a safe and cosy haven.

Related house-names:
Nyth-bach (Little nest).
Nyth-cacwn (Hornets' nest).
Nythfa (Nesting place; Shelter).
Nyth-glyd (Cosy nest).
Nythle (Nesting place; Shelter).
Nyth-y-brithyll (The trout's nest).
Nyth-y-dryw (The wren's nest).
Nyth-y-frân (The crow's nest).
Nyth-yr-eryr (The eagle's nest; eyrie).
Nyth-yr-wylan (The gull's nest).
Nyth-y-wennol (The swallow's nest).
Nyth-y-wiwer (The squirrel's nest; Drey).

O

Ochr-y-bryn (The hillside).
This house-name describes the general location of the dwelling.

Related house-names:
Ochr-y-cwm (Side of the valley).
Ochr-y-môr (The seaside).
Ochr-y-mynydd (The mountainside).

Oddi-ar-y-llyn (Away from the lake).
The house-name is explicit. The location is defined and the property can be identified.

Related house-name:
Oddi-ar-y-twmpath (Away from the hillock).

Odyn, (Yr) ((The) Kiln).
A lime-kiln flourished formerly on this site and the occupants are aware of this historic fact.
Related house-name:
Odyn-foel (Bare kiln).

Oerfa (Cool or shaded place).
The summer season can often be hot and humid in many parts of the country. Here the householders declare that they reside in a cool shaded spot.

Ogof, (Yr) ((The) Cave).
This house-name refers back to the time when man had found his first permanent home. The present householders reminds us of this salutary fact.
Related house-name:
Ogof ludw (Cave of ashes).

Olchfa, Yr (The washing place).
This historic name records the 'stopping place' customarily used in the past by barefoot traders on their way to market. Face and feet would be washed in the wayside stream and footwear worn for the final approach. Here is an example of a place-name transferred as a house-name due to personal ties of the householders with Yr Olchfa – an area west of Swansea City.

Olwyn, (Yr) ((The) Wheel).
Usually a large cart or carriage-wheel rests beneath the

house-name signifying a close connection between the household and agricultural vehicles.

Related house-name:
Olwyn-ddŵr (Water wheel).

O'r diwedd (At last).
The householders have at long last achieved their goal. This must be the dwelling of their dreams and the house-name confirms it.

Oriel (Gallery).
The house-name suggests that the dwelling is used as a gallery *and* a house. The occupants have the privilege of viewing works of art in comfort and on their own hearth.

P

Pandy (Y) ((The)Fulling mill).
The house-name records the original designation of the building. Today it is a comfortable, domestic dwelling and the owners by using this name retain a link with its historic past.

Related house-name:
Pandy-coch ((The) Red fulling mill).

Pant, (Y) ((The)Hollow).
The dwelling is situated in the hollow and is sheltered from unwelcomed winds.

Related house-names:
Pant-dwfn (Deep hollow).
Pant-glas (Green hollow).
Also the name of a village near Clynnog, Gwynedd and possibly transferred as a house-name.

Pant-gwyn (White hollow).
Also the name of a district near Llangoedmor, Ceredigion and possibly transferred as a house-name.
Pant-haul (Sun's hollow).
Pant-hyfryd (Beautiful hollow).
Pant-mawr (Large hollow).
Also the name of a district near Llangurig, Powys and possibly transferred as a house-name.
Pant-tawel (Quiet hollow).
Pant-teg (Beautiful hollow).
Also the name of a parish in Monmouthshire and possibly transferred as a house-name.
Pant-y-betws (Hollow of the house of prayer).
Pant-y-blodau (Hollow of the flowers).
Pant-y-brodyr (The brothers' hollow).
Pant-y-cadno (The fox's hollow).
Pant-y-carw (The deer's hollow).
Pantycelyn (The holly hollow).
Pant-y-dderwen (The oak-tree hollow).
Pant-y-defaid (The sheep's hollow).
Pantyderi (The oaks' hollow).
Pant-y-drain (Hollow of the thorns).
Pant y fedwen (The birch-tree hollow).
Pant-y-garlleg (The garlic hollow).
Pant-y-gog (The cuckoo's hollow).
Also the name of a district near Llangeinwyr, Bridgend and possibly transferred as a house-name.
Pant-y-gwiail (Hollow of the twigs).
Pant-y-gwin (The wine hollow).
Pant-y-llwydrew (The hoar-frost hollow).
Pant-y-meillion (The clover hollow).

Pant-y-nos (The night's hollow).
Pant-yr-athro (The teacher's hollow).
Pant yr awel (Hollow of the breeze).
Pant-yr-hebog (The falcon's hollow).
Pant-y-rhos (The hollow of the moor).
Pant-yr-wylan (The gull's hollow).
Pant-yr-ynn (Hollow of the ash-trees).
Pant-yr-ysgawen (Hollow of the elder-tree).
Pant-y-seiri (The paved-walkway hollow).
Pantysgawen (Elder-tree hollow).

Parc Caradog (Caradog's park).
The house-name clearly identifies a particular person with this piece and parcel of land.
Related house-names:
Parc-y-bore (The morning's park).
Parc-y-dŵr (The water park).
Parc-y-felin (The mill park).
Parc-y-marchog (The knight's park).
Parc-y-wrach (The witch's park).

Patshyn (Patch of land).
The dwelling is located on a small piece or parcel of land. The occupants are content and revel in the fact that 'small can be beautiful'.
Related house-name:
Patshyn Glas (Green patch of land).
Also the name given to a parcel of land near Goginan, Ceredigion and to another in the parish of Mynachlog-ddu, Pembrokeshire, and possibly transferred as a house-name because of ties between the householders and Patshyn Glas.

Pellorwel (Distant horizon).
The view from the dwelling is impressive. It stretches to the far horizon and inspires the householders.

Pencnwc (Top of knoll).
The dwelling is well situated on the knoll and commands pleasant views of surrounding countryside.
Related house-names:
Pendraw (Far end; Furthest point).
Penffin (End of boundary).
Pen-ffordd (Top of (the) road).
Also the name of a village near Trefelen, Pembrokeshire and possibly transferred as a house-name.
Pengelli (Grovesend).
Also the name of two villages: one near Gorseinon, Swansea, the other near Llanfeugan, Powys and possibly transferred as a house-name.
Penhwylbren (Top of mast or flagstaff).
Pen-llwyn (Head of (the) grove).
Pen-lôn (End of lane).
Penmorfa (Head of (the)sea-shore).
Also the name of a village near Dolbenmaen, Gwynedd and possibly transferred as a house-name.
Pennant (Upland; Head of valley).
Also the name of a village directly south of Llanbryn-mair, Gwynedd and possibly transferred as a house-name.
Pen'rallt newydd (Top of the new forest).
Pen-rhiw (Top of hill).
Also the name of a village near Maenordeifi, Pembrokeshire possibly transferred as a house-name.
Pen-rhos (Head of moorland).
Also the name of a village near Raglan, Monmouthshire

and of another near Ystradgynlais, Powys. In addition, it is the name of a district in the parish of Llandrinio, Powys and possibly transferred as a house-name.

Pen-sarn (Head of causeway).

Also the name of a village near Carmarthen; Abergele, Conway; and Bryncir, Gwynedd and possibly transferred as a house-name.

Pentraeth (End of sea-shore).

Also the name of a parish and village in Anglesey possibly transferred as a house-name.

Pen-twyn (Top of (the) hillock).

Also the name of a village and district in Monmouthshire and that of a village near Gelli-gaer, Caerphilly and possibly transferred as a house-name.

Penyberth (End of the hedge).

Pen-y-bont (End of the bridge).

Also the name of a village near Llandegley, Powys and that of a village near Llanfynydd, Flintshire. Mention must be made of the town **Pen-y-bont ar Ogwr** – namely Bridgend (on the River Ogwr).

Pen-y-bryn (Top of the hill).

Pen-y-cae (End of the field).

Also the name of a parish and village near Wrecsam and that of a village near Ystradgynlais, Powys and possibly transferred as a house-name.

Pen-y-cei (Top of the quay).

Pen-y-coed (Top of the wood).

Pen-y-cwm (Head of the valley).

Also the name of a village near Breudeth, Pembrokeshire possibly transferred as a house name.

Pen-y-daith (The journey's end).

Pen-y-feidr (End of the narrow country lane).

Pen-y-gaer (Top of the fort).
Pen-y-graig (Top of the rock).
Pen-yr-allt (Top of the hill or wood).
Penyrheol (Top of the road).
Also the name of three villages: one in the parish of Eglwysilan, Cardiff; another in the parish of Pant-teg, Monmouthshire; and the third near Gorseinon, Swansea possibly transferred as a house-name.
Pen-y-waun (Top of the heath).
The name of a village near Aberdâr, Rhondda Cynon Taf.

Perllan-deg (Beautiful orchard).
The dwelling stands near a fruitful orchard, where the year is observed by the householders as the trees bud, leaf, flower and fruit in due season.
Related house-name:
Perllan Llywelyn (Llywelyn's orchard).

Perthi (Hedges).
The property has well trimmed hedges defining its boundaries and demonstrating the care bestowed generally on the dwelling.
Related house-names:
Perthi-aur (Golden hedges).
Perthi-crwn (Round hedges).
Perthi-teg (Beautiful hedges).

Plas, (Y) ((The)Hall or mansion).
This house-name usually suggests a dwelling *par excellence* with a sweeping driveway and formal lawns.
Related house-names:
Plas-bach (Small hall or mansion).

Plas-bardd (Poet's hall or mansion).
Plas-coch (Red hall or mansion).
Plas-gwyn (White hall or mansion).
Plas-isaf (Lower hall or mansion).
Plas mawr (Large hall or mansion).
Plas Medi (September hall or mansion).
Plas-newydd (New hall or mansion).
See: **Hen blas**.

Porth Angel (Angel's assistance).
The householders in this dwelling believe in angels, faith being the only necessary requirement in order to face all of life's trials and tribulations.

Porth-y-gogledd (The northern port).
With this house-name there is a strong feeling that a connection exists between the householders and one of the northern ports, such as Amlwch, Holyhead or Porthmadog.

Pwll-defaid (Sheep's pool).
The dwelling is situated near or in full view of the pool where the animals gather.
   Related house-names:
Pwll-deri (Oak trees' pool).
Pwll-du (Dark pool).
Pwll-eog (Salmon's pool).
Pwll-glas (Blue pool).
Also the name of a village near Rhuthun, Denbighshire, possibly transferred as a house-name.
Pwll-y-wrach (The witch's pool).
Pyllau-crynion (Round pools).

R

Rhandir (Portion of land).
The house-name states simply that the dwelling stands on a piece of land.
Related house-name:
Rhandir-mwyn (Land of minerals).
This is also the name of a village in the parish of Llanfair-ar-y-bryn, Carmarthenshire.

Rheidol (The River Rheidol which flows into Cardigan bay at Aberystwyth, Ceredigion).
This is an example of the name of a river transferred as a house-name due to the close ties forged between the householders and the River Rheidol.

Rhiw, (Y) ((The)Hill).
The hill is the dominating feature in the locality and the dwelling is situated on it, hence the house-name. It is also the name of a village near Aberdaron, Gwynedd.
Related house-names:
Rhiwaderyn (Bird's hill).
Also the name of a village in the parish of Graig, Monmouthshire.
Rhiw-felen (Yellow hill).
Rhiwlas (Green hill).
Also the name of a village near Llanddeiniolen, Gwynedd.
Rhiw Siôn (Siôn's hill).
Rhiw-yr-efail (The forge hill).

Rhodfa'r eos (The nightingale's pathway).
The dwelling's location is immediately below the nightingale's

nocturnal pathway to the stars and the occupants are thrilled by its song.

Rhos (Moorland).
The town and urbanisation are far from this location, and the scene is rural as confirmed by the house-name. The householders may have transferred the name of a village near Yr Allt-wen, Pontardawe, Swansea or that of another village in the parish of Llangeler, Carmarthenshire due to personal connections.
  Related house-names:
Rhos-awel (Moorland breeze).
Rhos-ddu (Black moorland).
This is also the name of a district near Wrecsam, possibly transferred as a house-name due to family ties with that district.
Rhos-deg (Beautiful moorland).
Rhos-dirion (Gentle moorland).
Rhos-fach (Small moorland).
Rhos-fawr (Large moorland).
Also the name of a village in the parish of Llannor, Gwynedd and transferred as a house-name due to personal ties.
Rhos-goch (Red moorland).
Also the name of a village near Rhos-y-bol, Anglesey.
Rhos-helyg (Willow moorland).
Rhosydd (Moorlands).
Rhos y deri (The oaks' moorland).

Rhosyn-mynydd (Mountain rose; Peony).
Flowers fascinate many people. A favourite with the householders is the peony.

Rhuo'r gwynt (The wind's roar).
Westerlies (Force 6-7) frequently batter the Welsh coast. With this house-name the householders record the wind's sound.

Rhyd (Ford).
The dwelling is situated near a ford and the house-name confirms the location. Also this is the name of a village near Maentwrog, Gwynedd and possibly transferred as a house-name.
Related house-names:
Rhyd-aderyn (Bird ford).
Rhyd-adlais (Echo ford).
Rhyd-awel (Breeze ford).
Rhyd-deg (Beautiful ford).

Rhyddid (Freedom).
Implicit are the questions raised by this house-name. Is it freedom from tyrrany at home or abroad? Is it a declaration of the state that exists within the four walls of the dwelling? It could well be a desire to share the aspirations of the French, with their strident cry of: *Liberté! Egalité! Fraternité!* (Freedom! Equality! Brotherhood!).

Rhyd-fawr (Large ford).
The house-name confirms that the dwelling is in the immediate vicinity of a large ford.
Related house-names:
Rhydfelen (Yellow ford).
Rhyd-hir (Long ford).
Rhyd-lydan (Broad ford).

Rhyd-wen (White ford).
Also a district in the parish of Cwarter Bach, Gwynedd.
Rhyd-y-bont (The bridge ford).
Rhyd-y-carw (The deer's ford).
Rhyd y colomennod (The pigeons' ford).
Rhyd-y-defaid (The sheep's ford).
Rhydyfelin (The mill ford).
Rhyd-y-fwyalchen (The blackbird's ford).
Rhyd-y-geifr (The goats' ford).
Rhyd-y-gof (The blacksmith's ford).
Rhyd-y-gors (The marsh ford).
Rhyd-y-gwin (The wine ford).
Rhyd-y-meudwy (The hermit's ford).
Rhyd-y-pennau (Ford of the hilltops).
This is also the name of a district in Cardiff and a village in the parish of Tirmynach, Ceredigion.
Rhyd y pererinion (The pilgrims' ford).
Rhyd-yr-arian (The silver ford).
Rhyd-yr-efail (The forge ford).
Rhyd-y-wrach (The witch's ford).
Rhyd-yr hwyaid (The ducks' ford)

S

Saer-coed (Carpenter).
This is a plain straightforward notice. The house-name proclaims that a carpenter lives there.

Sain-yr-ehedydd (The lark's song).
The dwelling sits in an idyllic rural setting and the occupants are enchanted by the lark's singing.

Related house-name:
Sain-yr-eos (The nightingale's song).

Sarnau (Stone-paved walkways).
The existence of stone-paved pathways near the dwelling is seen as a significant feature and used as the house-name.
Related house-name:
Sarnau-gwynion (White stone-paved walkways).

Sawdde (The name of a river).
This is an example of a river's name transferred as a house-name due to the householders' close links at some stage in the past with this tributary of the River Tywi.

Seibiant (Rest; leisure).
This house-name suggests a complete antidote to the 'all work and no play . . .' syndrome. Proper rest can rejuvenate mind and body.

Seintwar (Sanctuary).
In addition to providing shelter from wind, rain and cold, the ideal home offers sanctuary from the storms and vicissitudes of daily living.

Seren-y-bore (Venus – the planet that appears as the morning (and evening) star).
Beginnings are important. The householders regard the observance of Venus at the start of the morning as a good omen for the rest of the day.
Related house-name:
Seren glaer (Bright star).

Sibrwd-y-dail (Whisper of the leaves).
Trees abut the dwelling and in summer and early autumn the sound of the wind in the trees is pleasing to the occupants.
Related house-names:
Sibrwd-y-gwynt (Whisper of the wind).
Sibrwd-y-môr (Murmur of the sea).

Simnai-tal (Tall chimney).
Buildings with distinguishing features are easy to identify. This dwelling has a tall chimney.

Siriol-fan (Happy place).
This house-name sets out the aim and intention of the occupants – to live in a happy environment.

Sisial-y-gwynt (Whisper of the wind).
The location is a favourable one. The dwelling's occupants hear only the whispering wind.
Related house-name:
Sisial-yr-awel (Whisper of the breeze).

Si-yr-afon (Murmur of the river).
The dwelling stands near the slow moving river and the householders find its sound comforting.

Sŵn aderyn (Bird's song).
The householders enjoy the song of a bird and name their house accordingly.
Related house-names:
Sŵn-y-brain (Cawing of the crows).
Sŵn-y-coed (Creaking of the trees).
Sŵn-y-dail (Rustle of the leaves).

Sŵn-y-don (Murmur of the wave).
Sŵn-y-dŵr (Murmur of the water).
Sŵn-y-gân (Sound of the song).
Sŵn-y-gloch (Sound of the bell).
Sŵn-y-gwynt (Sound of the wind).
Sŵn-y-môr (Sound of the sea).
Sŵn-y-nant (Murmur of the stream).
Sŵn-y-plant (Sound of the children).
Sŵn-yr-afon (Sound of the river).
Sŵn-yr-wylan (Cry of the gull).

Swyn-y-gwynt (The wind's (magic) charm).
The sound of the wind around the dwelling casts a spell on the unsuspecting householders.
Related house-names:
Swyn-y-nant (The stream's (magic) charm).
Swyn-yr-awel (The breeze's (magic) charm).
Swyn-y-wawr (The dawn's (magic) charm).

Sychbant (Dry hollow).
Not all hollows are dry. This house-name proclaims a dry site where the dwelling stands. The householders are fortunate.

Sylfaen (Foundation).
A solid foundation is a prerequisite of an idyllic home. The house-name infers this maxim.

T

Talar (Headland).
The unique location of the dwelling figures in the house-name.

Related house-names:
Talar-deg (Beautiful headland).
Talar-goch (Red headland).
Talar-wen (White headland).

Tal-y-bont (End of the bridge).
The location of the dwelling is well defined by the house-name. It is also the name of five villages in: Gwynedd (2); Ceredigion (1); Powys (1) and Conwy (1).
Related house-names:
Tal-y-llyn (End of the lake).
Also the name of a village, district and lake near Abergynolwyn, Gwynedd and that of a village near Brecon, Powys and possibly transferred as a house-name.
Tal-y-waun (End of the moor).
Also a village near Abersychan, in Torfaen County Borough and possibly transferred as a house-name.
Tal-y-wern (End of the alder-trees).
Also a village near Darowen, Powys and possibly transferred as a house-name.

Tanffynnon (Below (the) fountain).
The dwelling is well situated for a supply of fresh spring water, a great advantage in a market of continually escalating costs.
Related house-names:
Tanllwyn (Below a grove).
Tan-y-bryn (Below the hill).
Tan-y-castell (Below the castle).
Tan-y-dderwen (Beneath the oak-tree).
Tan-yr-allt (Below the woods).
Tan-yr-eglwys (Below the church).
Tan-yr-onnen (Beneath the ash-tree).

Tangnefedd (Peace).
This house-name may be a common form of greeting in the Biblical tradition: 'Peace be unto you!'

Tawelfa: Tawelfan (Quiet place).
Life's noise and bustle are counteracted here by the calm and tranquillity that pervades the home and its environs.
Related house-names:
Tawelfor (Calm sea).
Tawelfryn (Peaceful hill).

Tegfan (Lovely place).
'A thing of beauty is a joy for ever: its loveliness increases . . .' The householders rejoice in the dwelling's fair and beautiful setting.
Related house-names:
Tegfryn (Fine hill).
Tegfynydd (Beautiful mountain).
Tegle (Splendid place).
Teg-orwelion (Fair horizons).
Tegwch (Fairness).

Telynfa (Harp's place).
In this dwelling pride of place is given to harp and harpist.

Tir-bach (A small piece of land).
With this house-name the householders express the content of their Land Certificate: 'a little plot', yet put to good use.
Related house-names:
Tir-garw (Rough ground).
Tir-gwenith (Wheat land).
Tir na n-Óg (Land of eternal youth situated in the Celtic Otherworld).

Tir-paun (Peacock's land).
Tir-y-gof (The blacksmith's land).
Tir-y-tylluanod (Land of the owls).

Tlws-a-thwt (Neat and dainty).
A dwelling that reflects the endless care and attention lavished on it by the indulgent householders.

To-gwyrdd (Green roof).
This house-name is quite explicit. The roof is *not* of Caernarfon Red, nor of Porthmadog Blue, but could well be of Westmorland Green slates, descriptive and distinctive.

Trefor (Large dwelling: Large town).
This is an example of a place-name transferred as a house-name due possibly to personal ties between the householders and a village of that name: near Llangollen, Denbighshire; or of another on the Llŷn Peninsula, Gwynedd; or of one of among several on Anglesey.
　　Related house-names:
Tre-gof (Blacksmith's dwelling).
Tregwynt (Dwelling place of (the) wind).
Tre-hafod (Summer residence).
Tre-llyffant (Frog's dwelling).
Trenewydd (New town).
Newtown (**Y Drenewydd**) is a town and parish in Powys. The place-name may have been transferred due possibly to personal reasons of the dwelling's owners.

Tre-wern (Alder grove dwelling place).
This is also the name of a village north-east of **Y Trallwng** (Welshpool), and of two parishes all within the county of Powys.

Trem Enlli (Sight of Bardsey Island).
From the dwelling the view is of this small holy island off the tip of the Llŷn Peninsula, with its history dating back to the sixth century. Now uninhabited it has become a protected nature reserve. *See*: **Enlli**.
Related house-names:
Trem-y-castell (Sight of the castle).
Trem-y-dyffryn (View of the valley).
Trem-y-môr (Sight of the sea).
Trem-yr-afon (View or aspect of the river).
Trem-y-wawr (Sight of the dawn).

Tresi-aur (Laburnum; Golden chain).
The laburnum with its chains of golden-yellow flowers in spring has captivated the imagination of the householders and provided an appropriate name for the dwelling.

Trigfan (Abode; Dwelling place).
This straightforward, no nonsense house-name declares the whole purpose of the building. This is where the householders live.

Troad-y-llanw (Turn of the tide).
The dwelling in this maritime location enables the householders to ponder the maxim: 'Time and tide wait for no man', and to observe the regular ebb and flow on the seashore.

Troed-yr-allt (Foot of the hill or wooded slope).
The dwelling is located at the foot of a hill or wooded slope which is the significant feature used in the house-name.
Related house-names:
Troed-yr-Aran (Foot of Yr Aran mountain).

Troed-yr-enfys (The rainbow's end).
Troed-y-rhiw (Foot of the hill).
It is also the name of a village near Merthyr Tydful and could be an example of a place-name transferred as a house-name due to personal ties of the householders with this particular village.

Tro'r afon (Bend of the river).
The view from the dwelling enables the householders to observe this particular aspect of the flowing river. The house-name confirms their pleasure.

Trwyn-swch (Tip of ploughshare).
The small piece of land on which the dwelling stands is shaped like a poughshare, that is, triangular, and this accounts for the house-name.

Trysor (Treasure).
The householders rightly state that their home is their treasure. Today's escalating housing market confirms their view.

Tu hwnt i'r afon (On the other side of the river).
To the disorientated, it appears as a helpful house-name. The dwelling may be found on the *other* side of the river.

Tŷ Aaron (Aaron's house).
This is a straightforward house-name incorporating the owner's name or that of a previous owner.
 Related house-names:
Tŷ Angel (Angel's house).
Tŷ-ar-y-bryn (House on the hill).
Tŷ-brith (Grey or mottled house).

Tŷ-calch (Whitewashed house).
Tŷ-canol (Middle house of terrace).
Tŷ Capel (Chapel house).
Tŷ Ceredig (Ceredig's house).
Tŷ-cerrig (House of stones).
Tŷ-clyd (Cosy house).
Tŷ-coch (Red house).
Also the name of a district on the west side of the City of Swansea possibly transferred as a house-name.
Tŷ-cornel (Corner house).
Tŷ-croes (Cross house).
Also the name of a village near Rhydaman (Ammanford), Carmarthenshire possibly transferred as a house-name.
Tŷ-cyntaf (First house (on the way)).
Tyddewi (St. David's).
The smallest cathedral city in the United Kingdom. The name is frequently transferred as a house-name.
Tyddyn (Homestead; Smallholding; Small farm).
This house-name is plain and straightforward and refers to the dwelling, outbuildings and the surrounding land.
Tyddyn-bach (Small homestead; Smallholding; Small farm).
Tyddyn-blawd (Flour homestead).
Tyddyn-cynnal (Supporting homestead).
Tyddyn-difyr (Pleasing homestead).
Tyddyn Fadog (Madog's homestead).
Tyddyn-gwyn (White homestead).
Tyddyn haul ((The) sun's homestead).
Tyddyn-isaf (Lowest homestead).
Tyddyn-mawr (Huge homestead).
Tyddyn-mêl (Honey homestead).
Tyddyn Ni (Our homestead).

Tyddyn Rhyddid (Freedom's homestead).
Tyddyn Ronw (Ronw's homestead).
Tyddyn-tecaf ((The) most beautiful homestead).
Tyddyn-teg (Beautiful homestead).
Tyddyn-uchaf (Highest homestead).
Tyddyn-y-bwlch (Homestead of the pass).
Tyddyn-y-cefn (Homestead of the hillside).
Tyddyn-y-celyn (The holly homestead).
Tyddyn-y-ddôl (The meadow homestead).
Tyddyn-y-dewin (The sorcerer's homestead).
Tyddyn-y-garreg (The rock homestead).
Tyddyn-y-gwynt (The wind's homestead).
Tyddyn-y-paun (The peacock's homestead).
Tyddyn-y-pistyll (Homestead of the spring).
Tyddyn-y-rhyd (Homestead of the ford).
Tyddyn y waun (Homestead of the moorland).
Tyddyn-y-wrach (The witch's homestead).
Tŷ-del (Pretty house).
Tŷ-derwen (Oak-tree house).
Tŷ-draenog (Hedgehog's house).
Tŷ-draw (Yonder house).
Tŷ-du (Black or dark house).
Tŷ Elfed (Elfed's house).
Tŷ-fry (House above; House aloft).
Tŷ fy Nain (My Grandmother's house).
Tŷ-glas (Blue house; Green house).
Tŷ-glöyn-byw (Butterfly house).
Tŷ-gof (Blacksmith's house).
Tŷ-gwyddfid (Honeysuckle house).
Tŷ-gwyn (White house).
Tŷ-helyg (Willow house).

Tŷ-hen (Old house).

Also the name of a village due north of Aberdaron, Llŷn Peninsula possibly transferred as a house-name.

Tŷ-heulog (Sunny house).
Tŷ-hir (Long house).
Tŷ-hydref (Autumn house).
Tŷ-hyll (Ugly house).
Tŷ-isaf (Lowest house (in valley)).
Tŷ-llonydd (Peaceful house).
Tŷ-llwyn (Grove house).
Tŷ Mair (Mair's house).
Tŷ-mawr (Large house).
Tŷ Mehefin (June house).
Tŷ-meini (House of stones).
Tŷ-melin (Mill house).
Tŷ-melyn (Yellow house).
Tŷ-môr (Sea house).
Tŷ-mynydd (Mountain house).
Tŷ Myrddin (Myrddin's house).
Tŷ-nant (Stream house).

Also, the name of a village near Cerrigydrudion, Conwy, and of another south-east of Llanuwchlyn, Gwynedd possibly transferred as a house-name.

Ty'n celyn (Homestead or smallholding in (the) holly bushes).
Tyn cwm (Homestead in (the) valley).
Tyn dolau (Homestead in the meadows).
Tynewydd (New house).

Also, the name of a village in the County Borough of Rhondda Cynon Taf transferred as a house-name due to personal ties of the householders.

Tŷ Ni (Our house).

Ty'nllwyn (Homestead in (the) grove).
Ty'nlôn (Homestead in (the) lane).
Also, the name of a district near Bodwrog, Anglesey and of another near Llandwrog, Gwynedd possibly transferred as a house-name.
Tyn'rallt ((The) homestead on the hill).
Tyn'reithin ((The) homestead in the gorse).
Also, a district in the parish of Caron-is-clawdd, Ceredigion possibly transferred as a house-name.
Tyn-sietyn (Homestead in (the) hedge).
Tyn-tyle (Smallholding on (the) hill).
Tyn-y-bedw (Smallholding in the birch-trees).
Tyn-y-berllan (Smallholding in the orchard).
Tyn-y-bryn (Smallholding on the hill).
Tyn-y-caeau (Smallholding in the fields).
Tyn-y-coed (Smallholding in the woods).
Tyn-y-cornel (The corner smallholding).
Tyn-y-drain (Smallholding in the thorns).
Tyn-y-ffordd (Smallholding of the road).
Also, the name of a district near Cwmrheidol, Ceredigion possibly transferred as a house-name.
Tyn-y-ffos (Smallholding of the ditch or dyke).
Tyn-y-fron (Smallholding on the hillside).
Tyn-y-graig (Smallholding on the rock).
Tyn-y-groes (Smallholding on the crossroads).
Also, the name of a village near Caerhun, Conwy possibly transferred as a house-name.
Tyn-y-grug (Smallholding in the heather).
Tyn-y-llwyn (Smallholding in the bush).
Tyn-y-lôn (Smallholding in the lane).
Tyn-y-maen (Smallholding on the rock).

Tyn-y-maes (Smallholding in the field).
Also, the name of a village near Llanllechid, Gwynedd possibly transferred as a house-name.
Tyn-y-mynydd (The mountain smallholding).
Tyn-y-pant (Smallholding in the hollow).
Tyn-y-pwll (Smallholding of the pool).
Tyn-y-rhedyn (Smallholding in the bracken).
Tyn-y-waun (Smallholding on the moor).
Tyn-y-weirglodd (Smallholding in the meadow).
Tyn-y-wern (Smallholding in the alder-trees).
Tŷ-olaf (Last house (on the road)).
Tŷ'r ardd (The garden house).
Tŷ'r bont (The bridge house).
Tŷ'r Capten (The Captain's house).
Tŷ'r celyn (The holly house).
Tŷ'r efail (The forge house).
Tŷ'r felin (The mill house).
Tŷ'r gof (The smith's house).
Tŷ'r melinydd (The miller's house).
Tŷ'r rhos (The moor house).
Tŷ'r iet (The gate house).
Tŷ'r llan (The church house).
Tŷ'r porthmon (The drover's house).
Tŷ'r Teulu (The Family's house).
Tŷ'r wennol (The swallow's house).
Tŷ'r winllan (The vineyard house).
Tŷ'r ysgol (The school house).
Tŷ-siriol (Happy house).
Tŷ Tad-cu (Grandfather's house – S. Wales).
Tŷ Taid (Grandfather's house – N. Wales).
Tŷ-talcen (End house of terrace).
Tŷ-to-gwellt (Thatched house or cottage).

Tŷ-twt (Dainty house).

Tŷ-pica (House with sharp, pointed roof).

Tŷ unnos (A cottage built overnight on common land and conferring the right of residency on the builder).

Tŷ-wrth-y-ffynnon (House near the fountain).

Tŷ-wrth-y-glwyd (House near the gate).

Tŷ-wrth-yr-eglwys (House near the church).

Tŷ-yfory (Tomorrow's house).

U

Uchelder (High place).

The house-name reveals the dwelling's location. It is situated well above the other properties.

Related house-names:

Ucheldir (Highland; Upland).

Ucheldre (High homestead).

Also the name of a district: one in Powys and one in Gwynedd possibly transferred as a house-name.

Uchelfa (High place; High ground).

Uwch-afon (Above a river).

Situation frequently governs the choice of house-name and gives the location clearly.

Related house-names:

Uwchlaw'r coed (Above the woodland).

Also the name of a region near Llanwnnog, Powys possibly transferred as a house-name.

Uwchlaw'r ffynnon (Above the spring).

Uwchlaw'r rhos (Above the moorland).

Uwchmynydd (Above mountain).
Also the name of a region near Aberdaron, Gwynedd possibly transferred as a house-name.
Uwch-y-coed (Above the woodland).
Also the name of a region near Penegoes, Powys possibly transferred as a house-name.
Uwch-y-don (Above the wave).
Uwchygarreg (Above the stone).
Also the name of a parish in Powys possibly transferred as a house-name.
Uwch-y-graig (Above the rock).
Uwch-y-llanw (Above the tide).
Uwch-y-niwl (Above the mist).
Uwch-yr-Hafod (Above the Summer Residence).

Uncorn (One chimney-stack).
This dwelling's notable feature is that it has but *one* chimney-stack, whereas other dwellings in the locality have at least two. Times have changed since the building was completed.

W

Waun-coed (Wooded moorland).
The dwelling overlooks a wooded region of moorland. The householders have incorporated the view in the house-name.
Related house-names:
Waun-crychydd (Heron's low-lying marshy ground).
Waun-ddu (Black moorland).
Waunfach (Small moorland).
Waunfawr (Large moorland).
It is also the name of both a parish and village in Gwynedd,

and that of a village near Aberystwyth, Ceredigion possibly transferred as a house-name.

Waun-ffynhonnau (Moorland of springs).

Waun-gron (Round moorland).

It is also the name of a village near the City of Swansea and of another near Pontarddulais, Swansea possibly transferred as a house-name.

Waunmeirch (Stallions' moorland).

Waun-wen (White moorland).

It is also the name of a district in Swansea City possibly transferred as a house-name.

Waun-y-frân (The crow's moorland).

Waun-y-mynach (The monk's moorland).

Also the name of a common near Llan-wern, Powys possibly transferred as a house-name.

Waun-piod (Magpies' moorland).

Waun-yr-wylan (The gull's moorland).

Wern-cornicyll (Lapwing's alder-marsh).

The dwelling provides a good observation post and the householders delight to note how both tree and bird thrive on wet marshy ground.

Related house-names:

Wern-deg (Beautiful alder-tree).

Wernfawr (Large alder-grove).

Wern-felen (Yellow alder-marsh).

Wernffrwd (Alder-marsh stream).

Wern-gron (Round alder-grove).

Wern-rhos (Moorland of the alder-marsh).

Wern-yr-wylan (The gull's alder-grove).

See: **Y Wern**.

Wrth-y-coed (Near the wood).
The house-name gives the dwelling's location immediately. The house's proximity to the forest is noted and both postman and visitor benefit.

Wybren-las (Blue sky).
Are the householders hoping for blue skies despite the dismal weather forecast or does their house-name remind them of halcyon days in summer when they first saw the dwelling?

Y

Y Caban (The cabin).
This house-name may relate to an earlier dwelling built on the site, 'of clay and wattles made'. It could also be that the householders wish to express that their home is small and unpretentious.

Y Cwt (The hut).
The householders declare that theirs is not a substantial property with vast accommodation but small and adequate, just sufficient for today's needs.

Y Cwtsh (The resting place; The hiding place).
This house-name hints at some of the requirements of the ideal home. It must provide a resting place for the busy, and hiding place for those who need to escape the storms and tempests of daily living.

Y Cyhudd (The shelter).
The dwelling provides shelter for the inhabitants, a home provides much more.

Y Ddôl (The meadow; The pasture).
The dwelling is situated near a large meadow. The householders observe some of the farm animals and the daily tasks of the husbandmen who look after them.

Y Don (The wave).
A maritime location is implied by the house-name. The occupants are obviously fascinated by the continuous wave motion.

Y Dreflan (The small collection of houses in the country).
This may well be the transference of an earlier place-name from the parish of Llanbelig, Gwynedd by householders with close ties to that parish.

Y Dychwel (The return).
Implied in this house-name are the householders' long years of absence from their native heath and the untold joy of returning to the hills of home.

Y Faenol: Y Faenor (Manor house; Mansion).
The house-name harks back to the time when **Y Faenor** was a former Welsh territorial and administrative unit comprising of a varying number of townships . . . The present dwelling may well stand on ground referred to above, whilst the householders remind the onlooker of the rich historical heritage connected to such a name.
  Related house-names:
Y Faenol-Fach (The small manor house).
Y Faenol-Fawr (The large manor house).

Y Fenni (Abergavenny).
This house-name reflects the ties that exist between the householders and the town of Abergavenny, Monmouthshire.

Y Freuddwyd (The dream).
The dwelling, in all its splendour, confirms that the householders' dream has been realised.

Y Gadwyn (The chain).
With this house-name the occupants insist that the home with all its attractiveness is the 'chain' that enriches and links the whole family together.

Y Gangell (The chancel; The sanctuary).
With this house-name the occupants expect that their home will offer security and the opportunity for peaceful meditation.

Y Garreg-wen (The white stone or rock).
A prominent geological feature is clearly seen in the vicinity of the dwelling. The householders capitalise on its distinctiveness. Who needs a post code?

Y Gilfach-glyd (The cosy nook).
This house-name prepares the visitor: on crossing the threshold the warmth and the welcome will be one.

Y Gorlan (The sheepfold).
A parallel is drawn by this house-name: as sheep return at nightfall to the safety of the fold so do members of the household journey back to the security of their home.

Y Gwanwyn (The Spring).

> *'Spring, the sweet Spring, is the year's pleasant king . . .'*
> (Thomas Nash).

Following the icy bleakness of Winter, the days begin to lengthen and many including the householders rejoice at the return of Spring. This house-name inspires them the year through.

> *'Nothing is so beautiful as Spring –*
> *When weeds, in wheels, shoot long and lovely and lush . . .'*
> (Gerard Manley Hopkins).

Y Lleiaf (The smallest).
The householders declare that the dwelling is the smallest in size in the neighbourhood and believe that small can be both adequate and beautiful.

Y Maen-melyn (The yellow stone).
The main feature viewed from the property is that of a large yellow stone. Its significance is featured in the house-name.
See: **Maengwyn**.

Ymdrech (Effort).
With this house-name the householders acknowledge that through their sustained effort they now possess a place of their own that suits them well.
Related house-name:
Ymdrech deg (Fair effort).

Ymyl-y-graig (Edge of the rock).
The dwelling stands on the edge of the rock and the views are superb, but not for the faint hearted.

Related house-name:
Ymyl-y-nant (Edge of the brook).

Yn-y-coed (In the woods).
This is a simple, straightforward house-name. It indicates that the dwelling is in the forest.

Yr Ardd (The garden).
There are two possibilities with this short house-name. It may indicate that the site of the present dwelling was originally a garden or that proud householders wish to draw attention to their horticultural skills.

Yr Engan (The anvil).
An obvious connection exists between the present dwelling and the smithy. A heavy anvil fronts the property. Was this the site on which the village smith once wrought his trade?

Yr Haf (The Summer).
> *'Sumer is icumen in Lhude sing cuccu!'*
>
> (*Cuckoo Song*, c.1250, Anon)

Surely this must be everyone's favourite season when the days are long and the sun bright overhead. The householders believe so.
See: **Y Tymhorau**.

Yr Hendy (The old house).
The house-name claims that the dwelling (or part of it) is very old. Only the title deeds can confirm this. Perhaps the householders hail from the Carmarthenshire village of **Yr Hendy** near the county boundary and Pontarddulais, Swansea and have brought the name with them as a linguistic souvenir.

Related house-names:
Yr hen-efail (The old smithy).
Yr hen-fasnachdy (The old business premises; The old shop).
Yr hen-felindy (The old mill-house).
Yr hen-felin-wynt (The old windmill).
Yr hen-festri (The old vestry).
Yr hen-feudy (The old cowshed or byre).
Yr hen-ficerdy (The old vicarage).
Yr hen-lythyrdy (The old post office).
Yr hen-reithordy (The old rectory).
Yr hen-stablau (The old stables).
Yr hen-ysgoldy (The old schoolroom).

Yr Odyn (The kiln).
This house-name harks back to the time when kilns were frequent features on Welsh farm lands. There were drying-kilns used for drying grain and there were lime-kilns for burning limestone. The present dwelling may be near the site of one of these kilns.
Related house-name:
(Yr) Odyn foel ((The) Bare kiln).

Ysgubor-ddegwm (Tithe barn).
This house-name is reminiscent of the time in Welsh history when tithes were paid annually on farming produce: Corn, hay, cattle, sheep, wool, poultry, milk . . . to the 'alien' Church of England. Tithe barns were designated as collecting points for this purpose.
Related house-name:
Ysgubor-fawr (Big barn).
Ysgubor Ifan (Ifan's barn).
Ysgubor-wen (White barn).

Ystlys-y-coed (Side of the woods).
The householders provide the location of the dwelling: it stands at the side of the woods.

Ystrad (Floor of valley; Vale; Plain).
Situation is used in this house-name. The dwelling overlooks a gentle vale or plain. (**Ystrad** is a frequent component in many place-names.)

Y Tymhorau (The seasons).
The householders are resigned to the passage of time and welcome anew each season with its particular characteristics. *See*: **Y Gwanwyn; Yr Haf**.

Y Waun (Moorland, heath, marshy ground).
The dwelling is situated close to the moorland and the householders enjoy the peace and solitude of the rural setting. *See*: **Waun-coed**.

Y Wawr (The dawn).
In this dwelling the householders have great expectations, for they believe that they are not the people of today's noon but of tomorrow's dawn.

Y Wenallt (The white wooded hillside).
The dwelling stands on or near the wooded hillside and the house-name describes the location. *See*: **Allt-wen, Yr**.

Y Wern (The alder-tree; The alder-grove; The alder- marsh).
The house-name confirms the view observed from the dwelling, that is, the tall, fine alder-tree, lover of marshy ground and renowned for its water-resistant wood. It is also

the name of a village near Selattyn, Shropshire, possibly transferred as a house-name.
Related house-names:
Y Wern-ddu (The black alder-marsh).
Y Wern-wen (The white alder-marsh).

Y Whît (The whistle).
Sounds are frequently referred to in many Welsh house-names: **Cân-y-gwynt, Cân-y-môr, Cân-yr-afon, Cân-yr-eos, Cri'r Wylan, Murmur-y-nant, Sŵn-y-plant . . .**
In this example the householders hear the intermittent whistle of the wind beneath the eaves of the dwelling.

Y Winllan (The vineyard).
Somewhere behind the façade of the dwelling there lies a plantation of grape-vines specially selected to withstand the vagaries of our Welsh climate. The householders are informative and enterprising!

A SHORT INTRODUCTION TO WELSH PRONUNCIATION

WELSH is the envy of many languages, in as much as it has a standardized pronunciation. Each letter in the alphabet, with the exception of **y**, has but one sound value. Thus Welsh texts may be read phonetically from the very start, once the learner has mastered the essentials. With the availability of suitable broadcasts on radio: Radio Cymru (VHF 92-95; 96.8), Radio Wales (882 KHz MW), local stations such as Sain Abertawe (1170 MW), Radio Ceredigion (VHF 96.9, 103.3), Radio Maldwyn (397m 756 KHz); Television Channel S4C-Digidol; cassettes, records and CDs, the learner has an unprecedented opportunity of listening daily to the language 'in action' to confirm pronunciation, idiom and usage. Ideally, the learner should practice, where possible, regular conversation with a Welsh speaker.

In the table below, consonants, vowels and diphthongs are considered and matched with approximate sound values. There remains however one sound value for which no English equivalent exists, namely **ll** as in **Llanelli**. This is best attempted as **hl**!!!

Welsh Consonants	*Approximate equivalent sound*
b	as in **b**ad, **b**ed, **b**it, **b**ook, a**b**ide.
c	as in **c**at, **C**live, **c**ount.
ch	as in German: A**ch**tung! J. S. Ba**ch**.
d	as in **d**ig, **d**inner, pro**d**.
dd	as in **th**em, **th**en, **th**e dog, **th**ose.
f	as in o**f**, e**v**e, **V**olga.
ff	as in o**ff**, **ph**ysics, **f**ly.
g	as in **g**et, **g**ive, **g**rey.
ng	as in ba**ng**, so**ng**, wi**ng**er, bi**ng**o.
h	as in **h**air, **h**ot, **h**itch.
j	as in **j**am, **j**ar, **j**unk.
l	as in **l**ip, **l**ever, **l**ot, **l**agoon.
ll	best attempted as **hl!**
m	as in **m**u**m**bles.
n	as in **n**o, **n**ever, **n**ine.
p	as in **p**op.
ph	as in **f**ill, **Ph**illip.
r	as in Scots' pronunciation of **r**ash, **r**ed.
rh	even stronger than **r**, as **hr**!
s	as in mi**ss**, ki**ss**, hi**ss**.
t	as in **t**in, **t**op, **t**i**t**le.
th	as in **th**ick, **th**eatre, **th**atch.

Welsh Vowels	*Approximate equivalent sound*
a	as in **a**pple, m**a**n, **A**berdeen.
â	'**a**' sound value held slightly longer.
e	is in b**e**t, g**e**t, m**e**t.
ê	as the '**a**' sound in m**a**ne, w**a**ne.
i	as in gr**i**n, sk**i**n, w**i**n.
î	as in '**ee**' sound in sh**ee**n, w**ee**p.
o	as in p**o**t, r**o**t, t**o**t.

u	as in **y**ear, **y**east, **y**esterday.
û	'**u**' sound held slightly longer.
w	as in **w**ent, **w**ood, **W**illiam.
ŵ	'**w**' sound held slightly longer.
y	(i) as the '**i**' sound in d**i**n, k**i**n, sp**i**n.
	(ii) as the '**u**' sound in r**u**t, sh**u**t, spl**u**tter.
ŷ	as for (i) but held slightly longer.

Diphthongs are combinations of two vowels pronounced together under one stress.

Welsh diphthongs:

ai
ae
au
   The sound value resembles the **'ai'** in T**ai**wan, Shangh**ai**. Welsh words: M**ai**, m**ae**, c**au**, h**au**l, p**ai**d, Sb**ae**n, mam**au**.

âi
âu
   With **âi** and **âu** the sound value is similar to **âi** above, with the **â** sound slightly longer. Welsh words: c**âi**, gwn**âi**, dram**âu**, gwel**âu**, them**âu**.

aw
   Combine **'a'** as in **a**t with **'w'** as in **w**in. The sound resembles the **'au'** sound in M**au**-m**au**. Welsh words: **aw**n, d**aw**, br**aw**, c**aw**s, gl**aw**.

ei
eu
ey
   The sound value as in w**ei**gh. Welsh words: **ei**, **eu**, c**ei**, cr**eu**, dw**eu**d, ll**ey**g, t**ey**rnas.

ew	Combine **'e'** as in **e**nd with **'w'** as in **w**ind. Welsh words: bl**ew**, d**ew**r, gl**ew**, rh**ew**.
oe **oi** **ou** **ôi**	As the **'oi'** sound in c**oi**l, Hann**oi**, and as the **'oy'** sound in t**oy**, b**oy**. Welsh words: c**oe**d, bl**oe**dd, rh**oi**, d**ou**, d**ôi**.
öy	As in **oi** above, except with the stress on the **ö**. Welsh words: br**öy**dd, gl**öy**n.
ow	As in b**ow**l, gr**ow**n, m**ow**n. Welsh words: g**ow**n, rh**ow**n.
iw **yw** (i) **uw**	As **'u'** in t**u**ne, em**u**. Welsh words: br**iw**, m**iw**, s**iw**, **yw**, c**yw**, b**yw**, D**uw**.
yw (ii)	The sound value of **'y'** is like that of: (i) **'i'** in **i**nn, p**i**n, w**i**n – Welsh words: c**y**n, h**y**n, ff**y**n, gl**y**n, (ii) **'u'** in c**u**t, h**u**t, n**u**t – Welsh words: '**y**', **y**r, d**y**ma, t**y**nnu, cl**y**wed, h**y**wel, t**y**wel.
wy	(i) As in **we**. Welsh words: g**wy**n, g**wy**nt, g**wy**rdd. (ii) As in **wee**. Welsh words: ch**wy**s, g**wŷ**r, g**wy**s. (iii) As in (i) above, except that the **'w'** sound is more emphasised. Welsh words: c**wy**n, h**wy**, tr**wy**n, **wy**.

Accent falls on the penultimate syllable in polysyllables, for instance:

    cărreg   cerddŏrfa
    cŏsbi   gwrăndo
    llĕstri   Pontargŏthi
    măneg   pentrĕfi
    păder   llygŏden

Exceptions to this rule usually carry accents:

    iacháu, caniatáu, coffáu, nacáu, ar wahán . . .

GLOSSARY

This short glossary of Welsh words (nouns, adjectives, prepositions . . .) is by no means exhaustive. For a fuller treatment of the subject the Reader is referred to any good Welsh dictionary (titles are suggested in the Bibliography section).

Abbreviations

adj.	*adjective*
adv.	*adverb*
c.	*conjunction*
def. art.	*definite article*
f.	*feminine*
n.	*noun*
v.	*verb*
pl.	*plural*
pn.	*pronoun*
prep.	*preposition*
px.	*prefix*

A

aber *n.* estuary, confluence
aberth *n.* sacrifice
aderyn *n.* (*pl.* **adar**) bird
ael *n.* brow
aelwyd *n.* hearth; home
aethnen *n.* aspen
afallen *n.* apple-tree
afon *n.* river
ail *adj.* second
allt *n.* hillside; wood
amlwg *adj.* evident, visible
annedd *n.* dwelling place
annwyl *adj.* dear
ar *prep.* on
ardd *see* **gardd**
arhosfa *n.* stopping place
awel *n.* breeze

B

ban *n.(pl.* **bannau**) peak, crest, bare hill
banc *n.* bank, hillock
barcut *n.* kite
bedwen *n.* birch-tree
beudy *n.* cowshed
blaen *n.&adj.* point, end; source; uplands; first
blewyn *n.* hair; blade of grass
bod *n.&v.* residence; to be
bodlondeb *n.* satisfaction
brân, *n. (pl.* **brain**) crow
brig *n.* top; twig(s)
bro *n.* region, vale
bron *n.* hillside, breast of hill
bryn *n.* hill
bwlch *n.* gap, pass
bwthyn *n.* cottage

C

cae *n.* field
caer *n.* fort
caled *adj.* hard; difficult
cam *n.&adj.* step; bent, crooked
cân *n.* song
canol *adj.&n.* middle, centre
carn *n.* cairn; hoof
carreg *n.(pl.* **cerrig**) stone
cartref *n.* home
castell *n.* castle
cefn *n.* back; ridge
celli *n.* grove
celynnen *n. (pl.* **celyn**) holly
cerdd *n.* song, music
cerdinen *n.* mountain ash
Cernyw *n.* Cornwall
cesail *n.* armpit; nook, recess
cigfran *n.* raven
cil *n.* retreat
cilfach *n.* nook; cove
clwyd *n.* gate
clyd *adj.* cosy, sheltered
cnwc *n.* hillock
coch *adj.* red
coeden *n. (pl.* **coed**) tree
coedwig *n.* forest
colomendy *n.* dove-cote
corlan *n.* fold, pen
cors *n.* bog, fen
craig *n.* rock, crag
crib *n.* crest, summit, ridge
croeso *n.* welcome
cromlech *n.* a dolmen
crud *n.* cradle
cwm *n.* valley, glen
cwrt *n.* court
cwyn *n.* complaint, lament
cyfoeth *n.* riches
cyn *c.* as; *prep.* before; *px.* first, former, ex-
cysgod *n.* shade, shadow, shelter

D

dafad *n.* sheep
dail *see* **deilen**
dan *prep.* under
dau *adj.&n.* (*f.* **dwy**) two
dawns *n.* dance
deilen *n.* (*pl.* **dail**) leaf
del *adj.* pretty, neat
delfryd *n.* an ideal
delyn *see* **telyn**
derwen *n.* (*pl.* **derw**) oak tree
dim *n.* nothing, anything
disgwyl *n.&v.* expectation; to expect
diwedd *n.* end
dôl *n.* (*pl.* **dolau, dolydd**) meadow, pasture, dale
draen *n.* (*pl.* **drain**) thorn
dros *prep.* over
du *adj.* black; dark
dwrgi *n.* otter
dyffryn *n.* valley
dyma *adv.* here is/here are

E

Ebrill *n.* April
efail *see* **gefail**
efo *prep.* with
eglur *adj.* clear, obvious, bright
ein *pn.* our
eithin *n.* gorse
encil *n.* retreat
enfys *n.* rainbow
erw *n.* acre
esgair *n.* ridge
ewyn *n.* foam, froth

F

fach *see* **bach**
faenol *n.* manor house, mansion
fan *see* **ban; man**
fedwen *see* **bedwen**
felen *f.adj. see* **melyn**
felin *see* **melin**
felyn *see* **melyn**
ffawydden *n.* beech-tree
fforest *n.* forest
ffos *n.* ditch, trench
ffridd *n.* mountain pasture
ffrwd *n.* stream
ffynnon *n.* (*pl.* **ffynhonnau**) fountain, well
foel *see* **moel**
fron *see* **bron**
fry *adv.* above, aloft

G

gaeaf *n.* winter
galwad *n.* a call; vocation
gardd *n.* garden
garn *see* **carn**
garreg *see* **carreg**

gelli *see* **celli**
gilfach *see* **cilfach**
glan *n.* bank, shore
glas *adj.* blue, green
glesni *n.* blueness
glyn *n.* valley, glen
godre *n.* foot or bottom (of mountain, hill . . .)
goedwig *see* **coedwig**
gof *n.* blacksmith
golwg *n.* vision, sight, aspect
golygfa *n.* scene, view
gors *see* **cors**
gorwel *n.* horizon
graig *see* **craig**
grug *n.* heather
gwahoddiad *n.* invitation
gwâl *n.* lair, den
gwanwyn *n.* spring
gwar *n.* place just above and behind something, upper part, brink
gwawr *n.* dawn
gwe *n.* cobweb, web
gweddi *n.* prayer
gwen *f.adj.* white
gwên *n.* smile
gwenith *n.* wheat
gwennol *n.* swallow
gwersyll *n.* camp
gwesty *n.* hotel, inn
gwigfa *n.* forest, wood
gwinllan *n.* vineyard
gwylan *n.* gull
gwyn *adj.* white
gwyrdd *adj.* green

H
haf *n.* summer
hafan *n.* haven
hafod *n.* summer dwelling
hamdden *n.* leisure
hanner *n.* half
haul *n.* sun
hebog *n.* hawk
hedd *n.* peace
helygen *n.* (*pl.* **helyg**) willow
hen *adj.* old
hendre *n.* winter dwelling
heulwen *n.* sunshine
hir *adj.* long
hud *n.* magic
hydref *n.* autumn

I
iet *n.* gate
iorwg *n.* ivy
is *prep.* under, below

L
lan *see* **glan**
las *see* **glas**
llaeth *n.* milk

llain *n.* narrow strip of land
llais *n.* voice
llan *n.* church, enclosure
llawen *adj.* happy, joyful
llawenydd *n.* happiness, joyfulness
llecyn *n.* a small place
llety *n.* dwelling, abode
llun *n.* picture
llwyn *n.* bush
llys *n.* court

M
maen *n.* (*pl.* **meini**) stone
maes *n.* (*pl.* **meysydd**) field
man *n.* place
mawr *adj.* big, great, large
meddyg *n.* doctor
meillionen *n.* (*pl.* **meillion**) clover
meini *see* **maen**
melin *n.* **mill**
melyn *adj.* (*f.* **melen**) yellow
melys *adj.* sweet
min *n.* brink, edge, lip
moel *adj.&n.* bare; bare hill
môr *n.* sea
mur *n.* wall
murmur *n.* murmur
mynachlog *n.* monastery
mynydd *n.* mountain
mysg *see* **ymysg**

N
nant *n.* stream
nefoedd *n.* heaven
neuadd *n.* hall
newydd *adj.* new
niwl *n.* fog
noddfa *n.* refuge, shelter
noswyl *n.* vigil; evening
nyth *n.* nest

O
ochr *n.* side
odyn *n.* kiln
ogof *n.* cave
olwyn *n.* wheel
oriel *n.* gallery

P
pant *n.* hollow
parc *n.* park
pell *adj.* far, far-off, distant
perllan *n.* orchard
perth *n.* hedge, bush
pinwydden *n.* (*pl.* **pinwydd**) pine-tree
pont *n.* bridge
porth *n.* assistance; door
pwll *n.* (*pl.* **pyllau**) pool

R
rhiw *n.* hill, slope
rhodfa *n.* walkway

rhos *n.* moorland
rhyd *n.* ford
rhyddid *n.* freedom

S
saer *n.* carpenter
sain *n.* sound
seibiant *n.* interval
seren *n.* star
si *n.* murmur
sibrwd *n.* whisper
simnai *n.* chimney
siriol *adj.* happy, joyful
sisial *n.* a whisper
sŵn *n.* noise, sound
swyn *n.* charm, magic
sych *adj.* dry
sylfaen *n.* foundation

T
tal *adj.* tall
talar *n.* headland
tan *see* **dan**
tangnefedd *n.* peace
tawel *adj.* quiet, peaceful
teg *adj.* fair, beautiful
tegwch *n.* beauty
telyn *n.* harp
tir *n.* land, earth, ground
to *n.* roof
tre(f) *n.* town; home
treflan *n.* small town
trem *n.* look, sight
troed *n.* foot
trwyn *n.* nose
trysor *n.* treasure
tŷ *n.* house
tyddyn *n.* homestead, smallholding, small farm
tylluan *n.* owl
tymor *n.* season

U
uchel *adj.* high, loud
un *n.&adj.* one; same, one
uwch *adj.* higher
uwchlaw *prep.&adv.* above

W
waun *see* **gwaun**
wen *see* **gwen**
wern *see* **gwern**
wrth *prep.* by; to; because; since
wybren *n.* sky

Y
y, yr, 'r *def.art.* the
ymdrech *n.* effort
ymyl *n.* edge
ymysg *prep.* among
yn *prep.* in, at
ysgubor *n.* barn
ysgyfarnog *n.* hare

SELECT BIBLIOGRAPHY

DAVIES, Elwyn, *Rhestr o Enwau Lleoedd – A Gazetteer of Welsh Place-Names.* Cardiff: University of Wales Press, 1958.

JONES, Bedwyr Lewis, *Yn Ei Elfen.* Llanrwst: Gwasg Carreg Gwalch, 1992.

JONES, Francis, *The Holy Wells of Wales.* Cardiff: University of Wales Press, 1954 & 1992.

Llyfr Cyfeiriadau Post – Postal Address Book. Cymru 1 Wales 1. Royal Mail, 2000.

Llyfr Cyfeiriadau Post – Postal Address Book. Cymru 2 Wales 2. Edition H. Royal Mail, 2002.

PIERCE, Gwynedd O. *et al., Ar Draws Gwlad.* Ysgrifau ar Enwau Lleoedd. Llanrwst: Gwasg Carreg Gwalch, 1997.

RICHARDS, Melville, *Enwau Tir a Gwlad* (gol. Bedwyr Lewis Jones). Caernarfon: Gwasg Gwynedd, 1998.

SMITH, Peter, *Houses of the Welsh Countryside.* A study in historical geography. Royal Commission on Ancient and Historical Monuments in Wales. London: HMSO 2nd edn. 1988.

THOMAS, R. J., *Afonydd a Nentydd Cymru.* Caerdydd: Gwasg Prifysgol Cymru, 1938.

WILLIAMS, Ifor, *Enwau Lleoedd.* Lerpwl: Gwasg y Brython, 1962.

Dictionaries:

GRIFFITHS, Bruce & Jones, Dafydd G. *Geiriadur yr Academi – The Welsh Academy, English-Welsh Dictionary.* Cardiff: University of Wales Press, 1995.

LEWIS, Edwin C., *Teach Yourself Welsh Dictionary.* 3rd edn. London: Hodder & Stoughton Educational, 2003.

LEWIS, Edwin C., *Y Geiriadur Cryno – The Concise Welsh Dictionary.* Llandybïe: Gwasg Dinefwr Press, 2001.

Atlas:

AA 2004 Big Road Atlas BRITAIN. 13th edn. Windsor: *AA* Publishing, 2003.